PURSUING HAPPINESS

Pursuing Happiness

One Lawyer's Journey

DESIREE JAEGER-FINE

CAROLINA ACADEMIC PRESS
Durham, North Carolina

LIBRARY OF CONGRESS CATALOGING-IN-PUBLICATION DATA

Names: Jaeger-Fine, Desiree, author.
Title: Pursuing happiness : one lawyer's journey / by Desiree Jaeger-Fine.
Description: Durham, North Carolina : Carolina Academic Press, 2021.
Identifiers: LCCN 2021019277 (print) | LCCN 2021019278 (ebook) |
ISBN 9781531019518 (paperback) | ISBN 9781531019525 (ebook)
Subjects: LCSH: Law--Study and teaching--Psychological aspects. |
Law--Psychological aspects. | Happiness--Psychological aspects.
Classification: LCC K346 .J34 2021 (print) | LCC K346 (ebook) |
DDC 340.092 [B]--dc23
LC record available at https://lccn.loc.gov/2021019277
LC ebook record available at https://lccn.loc.gov/2021019278

Carolina Academic Press
700 Kent Street
Durham, North Carolina 27701
(919) 489-7486
www.cap-press.com

Printed in the United States of America

Toni
Forever and a day

Contents

Contents

Contents

Preface

I studied law in Germany and the U.S., and thus am educated both in the civil and common law traditions. The German legal and educational systems are quite different from the U.S. legal and educational systems, and I feel lucky to have experienced both. There are many apparent differences between European and U.S. methods of legal education, but the most striking for me was the prevalence of mental health problems in U.S. law schools. The pain and torment that I saw in my peers' eyes felt like a culture shock and a human tragedy. It seemed as if the toll on students' mental health was not only an accepted characteristic of law school life but that there was a sense of pride in the belief that law school must be a grueling and overwhelming ordeal to adequately prepare students for legal practice. Having learned of the suicide of a bright young law student, I decided to look into this problem with the sincerity that it deserves. I now work in legal education and recognize this issue both as an impediment to success and a failure to protect our future generation of lawyers.

This book is not meant to critique legal education but rather to serve as a refuge for law students. In this preface, I outline what I believe are the reasons for law student unhappiness. Subsequent chapters offer suggestions to help dismantle certain unhealthy thought patterns that education fosters so that students can find solace in and beyond the law.

Competition

We live in a tremendously competitive environment, and competitive success is seen as a source of happiness. Life is treated as a contest in which respect is to be accorded to the victor. We spend much of our lives competing to win at games without giving much thought to whether or not we want to play. First, many compete to get into a prestigious high school. Then we compete to get into a prestigious college, where we compete for grades. Then we compete for LSAT scores. Then we compete to get into a prestigious law school. Then we compete for law school grades, law journals, clerkships, and jobs. After years of conditioning, are we going to stop competing? Are we going to stop comparing ourselves to others? Of course not. We will keep competing—competing to bill more hours, attract more clients, win more cases, and earn more money.

We feel this struggle for success, just like our ancestors felt their battle for survival. The glorification of superhuman effort and achievement makes us believe that only a successful human being is worthy of having been born. We feel as if we are only truly seen when we outshine our peers. This combat mentality causes discord within us. Deep down, most of us want nothing more than to have a safe and reasonably comfortable life with meaningful work, a loving family, and caring friends.

Issue Spotter

Studying law has a natural tendency to produce discord. As law students, we are trained to look for and anticipate issues. We are trained to view life as a set of problems waiting to happen. If we cannot spot the issue in an exam, if we cannot anticipate problems when we draft a contract, we have failed. The world of a lawyer is a world of problems. This is underscored by the fact that law is an adversarial system. This notion is introduced early on in our law study, as appellate decisions form the mainstay of legal education, especially in first-year doctrinal courses. And as agents of others, much of our work is as advocates promoting particular positions, whether those positions are advocated in the courtroom or the boardroom. With its emphasis on conflict, this issue- and position-centered training compromises our natural zest and appetite for the beautiful.

Discipline

Legal education places a virtually singular value on rigorous, objective, analytic thinking, which minimizes the perceived utility of other kinds of thinking. Much of our unhappiness as law students is tied to the rigorous analytical approach inherent in teaching us to think like lawyers. This approach depletes creativity and compels us to value facts over imagination, rules over context, consistency over ambiguity, and rationality over emotion. It is no wonder that we begin to exhibit signs of distress during our studies given this method of thinking—coupled with the heavy workload; the crushing competition for grades, journal membership, clerkships, and other top jobs, and other external standards of success; as well as the Socratic method, which induces stress and exposes ignorance (or perceived ignorance).

The Good Fight

Many of us also experience a form of cognitive dissonance during law school. Many decide to pursue a career in law because of service-oriented values, values that dissipate during and are largely anomalous to law study. Due to insurmountable debt, many of us feel pressured into a career we might otherwise not have chosen.

For Our Future

The ambition fostered before and during law school places an undue emphasis on the future. Our mind is often ahead of both its time and its capacity. We are driven by promises, hopes, and assurances as a horse is driven by a whip. In the guise of professional development, we are trained to meditate on our shortcomings. We are continuously confronted with an image of ourselves as we ought to be, which is in continual conflict with who we are at the moment. This dissonance with self destroys the essential quality of life.

If all of this sounds hopeless, I promise that it does not have to be that way. We are more than competitive, success-hungry, and issue-spotting machines. We can be happy. It is time for a revolution!

PURSUING HAPPINESS

Inversion

The idea of writing a book about happiness for law students and attorneys came to me during a vacation in Cancun just weeks before the COVID-19 pandemic hit New York. It is one thing to write a book about happiness while you lie at the beach sipping fruity cocktails but quite another when you are locked at home, separated from your family by an ocean, and frightened about your health and that of those you love. New York City went into lockdown in March 2020, and my manuscript was due in December 2020. I was slightly discouraged, to say the least. How could I possibly say anything about happiness during such times? But what seemed like a good idea at the wrong time was actually a good idea at the perfect time. I had a lot more time on my hands for introspection and took the COVID lockdown as an occasion to ask myself this question: Am I happy?

This book is not based on scientific or other research but on my personal experience. I was never comfortable talking about emotions—we Germans tend to be reserved. In this book, however, I am brutally honest with myself and with you, which can sometimes be painful. I cannot offer anything else but my truth, which I have been forced to confront in working on this manuscript. Before I even started to write, I knew that this book would be just as much for me as it would be for you.

It is easy to tell others what to do. But each one of us needs to find her own way. I am sharing my journey in the hope that it will help you find yours. Do not be a second-hand person by merely trying to live out what I have told you. Use this book as a vehicle to discover something in and for yourself, something new, pristine, and original. I am no authority, just a friend sharing thoughts that I hope will spark and enable your very own revolution.

I hope to do this by suggesting a radical new look at life. Some of you may remember what it was like to open your camera's back and insert a film strip. Once the film was full, you brought the film to the photoshop and picked up your photos a few days later in a paper envelope. With your photos, you also received strips of photo negatives. Those negatives could be used to make more copies of the pictures. They are called negatives because the light exposure and colors in the actual photo are the exact opposite of the photo negative—a light and color inversion. Just as a photo and its negative are the same, "real" life and "negative" life are the same, with good and bad inverted.

Until now, I have been living a negative version of life. The things that I ran away from are necessary to find happiness. And conversely, many things which I thought were conducive to happiness turned out to be detrimental, or at the very least irrelevant. After reading this book, life will not have changed, but you may be able to look at the actual scene rather than its negative.

At first, you might not be able to see clearly in this new world. When you turn off the light in your room, your eyes need time to adjust. Little by little, you begin to see in the dark and navigate the room. Similarly, this new world may at first seem difficult to navigate, but if you give yourself time, your sight will adjust and what seemed dark is brighter than you could ever imagine.

The ideas expressed in this book may give the impression that I live as a hermit in the woods, spending my days cross-legged in contemplation, lighting candles, chanting mantras, and sipping tea. Nothing could be further from the truth. I live in Manhattan and work at a law school. I commute to work with my electric unicycle while listening to music. In the evening, I enjoy a drink, junk food, and Netflix. I do not do yoga or Pilates, although I do meditate. I also compete in Olympic-style weightlifting. I am in love with my life in New York City, the fast-paced, noisy gateway to both heaven and hell. I am fortunate to be able to enjoy the luxuries and conveniences the city has to offer.

Despite all of this, or perhaps because of it, I feel increasingly perplexed by how miserable many of us are. The way most of us live—myself included—strikes me as quite absurd. Law students and legal professionals in particular often work to the point of mental illness, addiction, or suicide, even though we enjoy conveniences our ancestors could only have dreamed of. How can this be?

Happiness requires an inversion so that we can see life in a different way—the right way. If we are seeking meaning where no meaning is to be found, if we cannot accept the inevitable, if we see only our commentary on life rather than life itself, if we are not thrown on our knees awed by life's bounty, how can happiness ever be found? In this book, therefore, the focus is on *unlearning* rather than learning, *non-doing* rather than doing, *reducing* rather than adding, *letting be* rather than cultivating, *letting pass* rather than grasping, *foregoing* rather than seizing, *letting go* rather than chasing. We will turn life upside down—and how wonderful it will be!

2

Can Someone Please Tell Me What to Do?

My childhood was peaceful, with no more than the average amount of struggle. My parents divorced when I was nine years old. They had purchased a restaurant and hotel which they managed together for the duration of their marriage. After the divorce, I discovered the enormous debt that the venture had accrued over the years. All of a sudden, I found myself living with my mom, my aunt, and my cousin in a studio apartment sponsored by welfare while my mother was juggling three jobs to pay off her half of the debt. She cleaned doctor's offices and worked in a hospital cafeteria. At night, she cleaned tanning studios. While doing all that, she completed high school so that she could become a nurse.

Paying the bills and feeding her two children was a tremendous struggle for my mother. I was very aware of her struggle, her fears, and the pressure of having to make ends meet. I was both sad for my mom and scared of life. I could not understand the purpose of all this suffering. How could anyone call this living? The feeling of senselessness was overwhelming and turned into frequent panic attacks. I barely managed to get through school. The divorce was the event that introduced my mom to her new life and introduced me to the disease that would accompany me for the rest of my life—depression.

The only way I knew how to cope with my depression was to charge ahead. So at the age of nine, I set out to understand the purpose of my life, a question that is still with me. It kicked off quite a journey—from being an actress, to a recording artist, a writer, a lawyer, and an entrepreneur. I bullied my life into submission trying to understand what on earth I was supposed to do to get rid of the pit in my belly.

Someone Much Smarter Than Me...

...asked himself the same question—what is the purpose of life—millennia ago. Aristotle, one of the greatest philosophers and scientists of all time, in his *Nicomachean Ethics*, embarked on a philosophical inquiry into the nature of the good life.

The purpose of Aristotle's inquiry was to discover the human good at which we should aim. Aristotle was not interested in a laundry list of things one needs, such as friends, health, and experiences that bring us pleasure. Instead, he searched for the highest good, which he assumed had two criteria: finality and self-sufficiency.

Aristotle went through the argument of elimination: Is the highest good honor, like receiving an award or good grades? Aristotle pointed out that this could not be the highest good for a human being since we seek recognition to confirm the idea of our own excellence. Is it excellence then? But we often seek excellence for something else, like wealth. So maybe it is wealth? Wealth, in particular money, is only good for what we can buy with it; money is not meaningful in and of itself, only for what it helps us get. We just have to think of inflation to understand that we value what money gets us, not money itself.

After proceeding in this manner, Aristotle arrived at happiness and decided that this was the highest human good. Most of the things we seek are to gain something else. We want good grades to get a good job to earn money. We desire money so that we can buy stuff. We want honor to feel better about ourselves. But happiness is a goal in and of itself. Aristotle noted that since happiness is not pointing to anything else like wealth or honor, it is the highest good. Happiness is both final and self-sufficient.

Aristotle actually never used the word happiness; instead, he used the Greek word "eudaimonia," which is often translated as happiness. This word can be more precisely translated as to "live well"—"*eu*" means good, "*daimonea*" means life. Some like to translate *eudaimonia* as flourishing, which seems closer to Aristotle's meaning than "happiness" as we understand it. The word "happiness" has been overused to the point where it is stripped of its meaning, but we use it here as a tool to help point us in the right direction.

3

What Are We Talking About Anyway?

If happiness is the highest good, we must understand what happiness is. This question has occupied great philosophers over millennia. So while I cannot offer a conclusive definition of happiness, I will define the state of being that this book is about, which I call "happiness."

I asked friends and family members how they define "happiness." But their answers only restated Aristotle's hierarchy problem. "I want to find love and build a family." We want to find love and build a family because we think this will make us happy. It still does not answer the question of what happiness is.

So what is that state of being called happiness that we all strive for? Is happiness the euphoria we feel when we win the lottery or when our sports team wins a championship? Is it the tingle in our belly when we fall in love? Is it the confidence we feel when we pass an exam with honors? Is it the sense of calm that we feel after a massage? Or is it the security that we feel when we sit in our parent's house, and our mom cooks dinner? While these are all beautiful feelings, they are not the state of being that I would like to explore here. These are temporary emotions, and they are heavily dependent on external forces. If happiness is the elation we feel when our sports team wins, we will live at the mercy of life's currents. True happiness must be more fundamental than that.

In law school and law practice, we become accustomed to breaking problems apart, analyzing them step by step, and solving them. We seek results. This approach cannot be applied to happiness. If we were to do this, we would follow a model that focuses more on functioning than on living. To exercise, sleep, and eat well are valuable suggestions, but these activities point merely to a method of maximum functioning. That is undoubtedly a valid pursuit, but to function well and to be happy are two very different things.

Although the idea of happiness remains elusive, there are a few things that we *can* say about happiness. First, happiness is not a result of something. Suppose it was, for example, the result of having a great job and financial security. Why are there so many who have exactly that but still are unhappy? Second, happiness is not the sum of parts. If happiness were the sum of, say, A, B, C, D, E, F, and G, and if we were to take D away, would we lose happiness? What happens if we remove C and D? At what point would happiness cease? Third, happiness is not divisible. We may use the phrase, "I am a little unhappy about this," but what does this even mean? Are we 30% unhappy and 70% happy? How does this 30/70 ratio feel in our body? It is impossible to tell because happiness is not a pie with individual pieces. What we mean when we say that we are a little unhappy is that we are irked by a circumstance. But that irk is just mud that does not affect true happiness. Finally, happiness has neither location nor center.

At the end of the day, happiness cannot be defined; it can only be revealed. Like a sculptor reveals a statue by removing stone, happiness must be revealed through the act of removing mud—certain ways of thinking and behaving to which we have come accustomed. Happiness, just like love, is so beautiful largely because it is undefinable. It is a state of being that is so singular that it cannot be measured, located, or defined but only felt. We can describe it, but words inevitably fall short; they can point in the direction but should never be mistaken for what they are pointing to.

We all carry within us the seed for happiness. This seed does not depend on anyone or anything to flourish; the seed is complete wherever and however we are now. The seed can blossom wherever and however we are. Happiness is our natural state—our baby nature—to which we can return whenever and wherever. In our society of addition, we add layer upon layer of muck and thereby obscure that state of being that lets us sleep like someone who has nothing to lose and nothing to gain. Clutter disguises what has been with us all along. The seed is incapable of being defined and is not something we can chase, yet it can be uncovered and returned to. Its simplicity is its greatest hurdle. Alan Watts said it best:

[S]uddenly, some very ordinary moment of your ordinary everyday life, lived by your very ordinary self, just as it is and just as you are...this immediate here-and-now is perfect and self-sufficient beyond any possibility of description.

4

Chasing a Ghost

If you want to get better grades, study harder. If you want to run faster, train harder. If you want to earn more money, work harder. If you want to be happy, do nothing.

Pardon Me, Mr. Jefferson

The Declaration of Independence is a sacred document for me—the articulation of the founding principles of the country I love. If I could travel back in time, I would ask Thomas Jefferson about his reference to the "pursuit of happiness." As a newly crowned American, I would ask the father of my country: "Do you really believe that you can pursue happiness?" Depending on the answer, I might add, "With all due respect, I think you are wrong."

I have measured my life by goals and collected them like others collect coins. Only recently did I come to know what it feels like to not pursue a goal. I arrived at the pinnacle of my life and had nothing left to long for. I could not handle this feeling. Without a goal, my present made no sense. Pursuing was the only thing I knew how to do. The meaning of everything I undertook was found in what it would bring forth. I lived for the future.

The quest that started at age nine sent me from one thing to the next. At first, I thought fame would make me happy, which did not separate me from many other children. Well into my teenage years, I imagined myself performing on stage, signing autographs, and giving interviews. Reality was so dull that it felt like a straitjacket from which I knew only one escape—my endless imagination. In a single hour, I could sell a multi-platinum album and steer a rocket ship to the moon.

Imagining did not satisfy me for too long, so imagination morphed into concrete goals. I stopped imagining something that was not, and started visualizing what would soon be mine. I gave up on my trip to the moon, but I gave birth to pretty much every other fantasy I nurtured.

Once Upon a Time in a TV Studio

One day I walked from an SUV to a TV studio where I would give an interview about my just-released record. Security guards in black suits on either side of me navigated my path. I occasionally stopped to sign autographs. While the guards pushed me gently towards the studio's entry, I bathed in the sound of my name. When I arrived in my wardrobe, I sat on my sofa and fell silent. This time it was not my imagination; I was twenty-one years old and this was my life.

This moment resembled my imagination in almost every detail. I say almost because it was missing something important—the feeling of fulfillment. It was exciting, for sure, and I was proud of what I had accomplished. But it left me with the same hollowness that I was desperately trying to run away from. I felt betrayed by the universe. Where was that moment of satisfaction? Where was that smile like that of the Buddha, full of wisdom and contentment? I spent my entire childhood in this moment and put all my faith in success, money, and fame. The feeling of emptiness was compounded by the fact that my life looked spectacular to others. The more they cheered, the lonelier I felt.

As I grew older, I acknowledged that I craved recognition and fame so that my life had meaning. I needed others to help me see what I could not see for myself—who I was and what I was sup-posed to do on this earth. I needed people to scream my name, and I needed them to ask for autographs when I bought my morning coffee. If others would look at my life and envy it, that must mean that my life was wonderful and, most importantly, that I was not a cosmic fluke but a special someone with a destiny.

My yearning for meaning and happiness drove my search for fame, power, and fortune. I sought it everywhere. I left the enter-tainment industry after ten years with the unshakable conviction that some other goal would do the trick. I thought that finding the right goal was the true challenge. Like a magician, I turned every fantasy into reality. No goal was denied. And with the fulfillment of each, I felt betrayed once again. The universe was playing a colossal joke on me. It supported my futile pursuits while laughing at my stupidity or waiting patiently for me to understand. I turned my life upside down over and over again, changing what I thought needed to be changed, chasing what I thought needed to be chased.

Only in the last year did I surrender to the fact that what I was doing was not working. I was treating thirst with salt water.

One does not need to be a psychologist to see that all I really longed for was to find meaning in my existence—not for its own sake but to be happy. So how do we pursue happiness? It turns out we do not.

Catching a Feather with a Fan

Aldous Huxley, born in 1894, was a writer and philosopher best known for his novel *Brave New World*. Huxley is also credited with formulating the "Law of Reversed Effort," which posits that as to certain tasks, the more effort we expend the less likely we are to succeed. If we are stuck in quicksand, for example, frantic movements will only hurt our cause. The vibrations caused by rapid body movements will turn relatively firm ground into even more quicksand. But if we relax, our body's buoyancy will cause us to float.

Happiness and quicksand have something in common. The more we chase happiness, the more we get sucked into despair. The philosopher Alan Watts referred to this as "the backwards law." It is the idea that the more we pursue feeling better, the less satisfied we become, as pursuing something only reinforces the fact that we lack it in the first place. Saying "I want happiness" or "I should try to be happy" is the same as saying "I lack happiness." As law students or professionals, focusing on future happiness merely underscores our unfortunate current state of affairs—by definition, one that is not happy.

"If you do this, then you will be happy" may be the most misleading statement of our time, yet it is the one I followed for thirty years. If you exercise regularly and eat well, you will be happy. If you find meaning in your work, you will be happy. If you save for retirement, you will be happy. Something to be gained implies that it lies in the future. When I look back to the times I thought I was happy, I see moments filled with promise and potentiality. I only seemed to feel a sense of satisfaction when the present was filled with promise for the future. Each moment in my life became an expectation. If I find happiness only in those moments that point to something else, how can I say that I am happy in and with this moment?

To chase happiness, to make it a goal, is to miss it. Happiness is not something to be sought, but something to be uncovered. At every moment, we can be completely content. Discord arises only when, through memory or expectation, thoughts about the past or the future muddle the present. If we proceed from a lack of faith in the truth that happiness is here, we already recede from it.

The past is gone, and the future has not yet arrived. The only time that is real is the present. To be happy, we must focus our attention on today. Tomorrow is just another today, after all. Happiness must be here today. If we seek happiness in the future, it will forever remain a mirage.

The Dog Behind the Radiator

Snoopy, my white and brown chihuahua, was an awesome little dog. She was just like me—full of life and slightly damaged. She abhorred loud noises, fast movements, and anything out of the ordinary. In the face of danger, she hid behind my radiator. There was not much room between the radiator and the wall, so once she was back there all I could do was wait for her to come out; there was no space for my arms to reach in and grab her. So while she was waiting behind the radiator, I was waiting in front of it. The definition of danger was broad for Snoopy—a sneeze, the accidental dropping of a book, or a louder than usual sigh was enough to send her behind the radiator. She was a fragile little girl.

Happiness is like Snoopy, both stable and fragile. Even though it can never be destroyed, it can hide behind the radiator. Once there, no amount of force can make it reappear. All one can do is stay calm.

Just like a campfire needs constant tending, happiness needs attention and care. For the fire to burn, it needs oxygen, space, and wood—but not so much that it will suffocate the fire. A fire needs much attention to get the flame just right, and we would never leave the fire unattended. Happiness requires the same level of commitment. If we treat happiness as our birthright, we do not regard it with the care that it deserves. As a birthright, it is just another item we think we have a claim to. We do not have a right to happiness; all we have is the right to be its guardian. It takes dedication to be happy.

Whenever something or someone muddles with my happiness, it is my happiness that I protect. But I, too, get thrown about by the currents of daily life. If there is a lapse in attention, my happiness retreats behind the radiator, where it waits with Snoopy for the right time to come back out. But that only strengthens my resolve. It is a dedication that I renew each and every day.

This tender caring and protection of our happiness is quite different from the forceful chasing to which we are accustomed. Try to chase Snoopy, and she ends up deeper behind the radiator. Nourishing and gentle coaxing, however, can bring her out. Snoopy was not a goal to be sought, but a friend to be taken care of. Happiness is no different. The philosopher Martha Nussbaum's comment on "the human condition of the ethical life" applies very much to happiness, as well: "[I]t is based on a trust in the uncertain and on a willingness to be exposed; it's based on being more like a plant than like a jewel, something rather fragile, but whose very particular beauty is inseparable from its fragility."

Just Quit!

I abhor giving up, and so does the culture and education that shaped me. We are conditioned to crawl across the finish line after a marathon, even if we are only inches away from a heart attack. Death after the race would make our accomplishment even more impressive; since we paid the ultimate price for our passion, we must have lived a fulfilled life. That is the ethos of our generation.

We should never give up on something because we do not want to put in the work. We cannot surrender because things get difficult. But there are situations in life during which giving in is the only way to succeed. This is a difficult proposition to accept since we are trained to never resign in the pursuit of our goals. But we do not give up because we do not want to exert effort; we give up because the effort is futile and moves us further away from happiness.

Effort implies power, force, and strenuosity, all of which lead us astray. Happiness can only be realized once we let go. Rather than moving toward something, we need to stand still; rather than speaking, we need to listen. Happiness emerges under the sole condition that we are not trying to make it happen. We must give up the notion of controlling the situation. Happiness is a state that the will is unable to bring about. Just like insomnia cannot be cured by willing oneself to sleep, happiness cannot be chased. It must happen by letting things be.

5

Is Happiness on Pause?

At the outbreak of the pandemic I did not work on this book, partly because I was distracted and partly because it felt cruel to talk about happiness amid devastation. The COVID infection rates in New York were high, and freezer trucks were lined up to accommodate dead bodies. My peers were locked up in shoe-boxed-sized apartments with windows that let in neither light nor air. Friends lost their jobs, their sanity, and their family members. How could I possibly write about happiness? What could I tell someone facing these tragedies about happiness?

Does happiness have to be suspended during a global pandemic or other tragedy? Am I a bad person if I feel happy while many around me are suffering? I was troubled by these questions. But no matter how much I tried to guilt myself into being unhappy, I could not find the off button. Of course, I was stressed, anxious, annoyed, scared, bored, and sad for those around me. But I admit that even at the peak of the pandemic, I remained happy.

I found myself in the confusing situation of being both sad for the people around me and being happy. I stopped asking myself whether this made me a bad person and started asking myself instead whether happiness and sadness were mutually exclusive. The answer at first seemed pretty straightforward: you are either happy or sad. When my friend tells me that he is sad, I "know" that he is not happy. But here I was feeling both happy and sad.

Does one have to feel one *or* the other? Was one of those feelings an illusion? For happiness and sadness to be mutually exclusive, I thought, they must be on the same seesaw. If one is up, the other is down, just like one either is dead or alive but never both. We leave Schrödinger's cat aside for now. Happiness and sadness, both being feelings, can be thought of as opposites.

But emotions are not mutually exclusive. Indeed, they can be quite messy—that is why we have therapists. Feelings are more akin to a fluctuating field of energy with peeks and crests, just like the ocean. Happiness and sadness are waves traveling through the same medium—feelings. In an ocean, one wave does not exclude another. One just has to stand at the beach and watch the many waves roll in. One wave is independent of any other wave, and when two waves meet, they pass right through each other. This happens with sound waves, too; when two people talk, you can hear both. One set of sound waves does not eliminate the other, but waves can interfere with each other.

Like waves, happiness and sadness may interfere with each other, but they are not mutually exclusive. It is therefore normal for someone to feel contrasting feelings at once. There can be a sadness wave and a happiness wave living in the same ocean of feelings.

The pandemic is an extreme example, but it is instructive for our everyday lives. There is always something or someone that annoys us, and inevitably we sometimes get stressed. But this has nothing to do with happiness. One can be frustrated by a law class, supervisor, or client while remaining perfectly happy. By reducing happiness to something so volatile that a single interaction can destabilize it, we turn a most momentous feeling into nothing more than a whim. Happiness is far more profound than these surface emotions. To confuse happiness with temporary emotions is to diminish it. To confuse happiness with a perpetual sense of elation is to miss the point altogether. Happiness may be a quiet harmony or a full orchestra, but either way, it is here. One has to choose to listen to it, which is not always easy. Happiness is not there but here, not sometime but now.

But even after I explained my feelings, it felt utterly inappropriate to admit to others that I was happy, let alone writing a book about happiness. As critical creatures, we feel compelled to judge whether someone is justified in feeling happy. I did not want my peers to think badly of me, so I complained with them. As a society, we judge whether and when it is appropriate to be happy, and we guilt others into stress and busyness. There are not many law students or lawyers who boast about their well-being and happiness. Mostly we hear our colleagues say things like "It is crazy. I am super stressed and too busy." We respond in such a way partly because that is how we feel, but also because we do not want to be outsiders. Law study and practice prides itself on being stressful and miserable; we feel that if someone is not suffering enough, she must not be working hard enough. We have come to equate a lack of stress with a lack of work ethic. We do not want to be judged as not working hard enough, so we join the complaints. But it is entirely OK not to be stressed; it is OK to be OK. We should not feel that we need to apologize for being happy and content. Happiness does not have to be on pause during a pandemic, during our legal education, or during our practice. Being a happy lawyer is not something to be concealed but something to be cherished, celebrated, and shared.

6

Trust

We have the ability to mold our existence, and it is this belief that consoled me when I shared a studio apartment with my mother, my aunt, and her daughter. "I can change this," was my mantra. "If I take charge, I won't be sleeping on the floor ever again."

So I went out into the world with little trust but with much determination to control. My experience had taught me that you have to take the reins and create the reality you wish for yourself. I am the master of my destiny, and if I am unhappy, only I am to blame. And so, in every situation, I took charge and controlled as much as I could to depend as little as possible on fate. It served me well. From the perspective of our cultural heritage, there is nothing wrong with this approach to life. On the contrary, it embodies the very ethos of the American Dream.

Legal education did not help me develop trust. To the contrary, I learned how to anticipate problems, see issues, and prepare for worst-case scenarios. The world of a lawyer revolves around issues that need to be foreseen, controlled, and solved. Trust has no place in it. After all, I would not tell the senior associate that I did not look at a draft contract because I trust that my counterpart perfectly embodied our agreement. But there comes a time outside the law school, classroom, or office when we need to let trust guide us.

What can be controlled is limited, and it takes wisdom to know what is controllable and what requires trust. To try to control the uncontrollable is a source of much stress and dissatisfaction. To add only what is needed, to reduce what is unnecessary, and to let life do what it knows to do best is the key to sound sleep at night.

Ultimately, we all long for trust—trust in ourselves, trust in the world around us, and trust that our lives have some fundamental meaning. We long for the kind of trust a sleeping child finds in his father's arms. No matter how loud it is around the baby, no matter how much the father moves, the child sleeps peacefully. The child knows that right there and then, everything is OK. Like the sleeping baby, at the end of the day, all we would like to feel is that everything will be OK—that our education will bear fruit, that our decisions will have made sense, that we will be surrounded by people we love and who love us. We need to trust the future, but even more importantly, we need to trust this very moment—that this moment is what it is supposed to be.

It might be difficult to conceive of trust when we do not know whether we can pass the next exam, find a job, handle a transaction, or pay our bills. But trust comes from no one else, attaches to nothing else, and longs for nothing. Only if it is free from circumstance can trust free us. Trust must be freed from fear; otherwise, it is mere clinging.

How do we acquire this kind of trust? We don't, because trust is not something you get but something you do. Trust is often taken to refer to something that springs from a source, like religious faith. But this type of trust, being tied to something else, is contingent. Trust must come from within ourselves. Trust is something that we do despite our surroundings. We can start trusting right now at this very moment. Nothing else is needed other than the act of trusting.

There are many things in life that we naturally trust because we recognize that we do not have any other choice. We trust that when we go to bed at night, we will wake up again in the morning. Without that trust, we would have a tough time going to sleep. We trust that when it rains, it will eventually stop. We trust that the sun will rise every morning and set every night. We trust that the earth will keep spinning and stay in its orbit and that gravity will keep us planted on this earth. We trust that the food we eat will not poison us, and that when we cross the street we will make it to the other side. Without this trust, we could not operate. Trust enables us to function; without it, we would be paralyzed.

Beyond these basic forms of trust we need additional trust to live happily. We must trust that life and death are OK. We must trust that even if we consider human life a cosmic accident, we still have meaning. We must trust that even if people run astray, at their core they long for love and peace just as we do. We must trust that our body does what it needs to do and that if it cannot anymore it will dissolve itself, because that is what it needs to do. We must trust that whatever adversity we face, we are endowed with the strength to handle it. We must trust that the kiss of a loved one contains everything we need to know about life.

This kind of trust requires the surrender of control because, in these realms, control is futile. This was a tough lesson for me to learn because control crept into every part of my life. Now, I am very slowly beginning to let go of control, and with this letting go, with more trust, I feel much better.

"Doesn't trust make one complacent and blind to injustice?" Yes, if taken to the extreme, because everything taken to extremes turns negative. Having no trust at all is the other end of the extreme and, therefore, harmful as well. Our society exchanges trust for control in most realms of life, and this causes anxiety and unhappiness. To live in a world that is perceived as not trustworthy is horrendously painful. "What can we do about the disorder and injustices around us?" We act when we can, and we trust when we cannot. Trust is neither the closing of the eyes to the pain of others nor the forceful pushing of life into a box. A happy life requires a balance of both action and trust, and it takes wisdom to know when to act and when to trust.

Swim With the Current

I used to encourage my students to find their own path and to use the road less traveled. Just as I was taught. We all fight to be unique, to be special, to be a separate, distinct "I" whose existence is justified by its uniqueness.

At the same time, I told my students how to behave in certain settings, what is expected of them as good citizens, good students, good lawyers, and good mentees. So my students tried both to be unique and to fit in. These messages contradict each other and cause confusion.

So what should we do? Swim with or against the current? Professional development encourages us to swim against the current and cites outstanding achievers who did just that—the rugged individualists. But to get to where we want to go happily, swimming against the current is not always necessary and can even be detrimental. Paddling against the current is exhausting and requires a tremendous amount of force. Have you ever tried to swim against an actual current? Doing so will slowly sap the life out of you. Often, we paddle against the current to run away from something we disapprove of or rebel against, such as a tradition or others' expectations. Then we add anger and frustration to the mix. How long can we keep up this explosive cocktail before we burn out?

To swim against the current implies that the current is flawed and should not be followed. But not every current moves in the wrong direction. Going with the current allows us to ride with nature. We can move with it like a surfer on a wave. A surfer does not push the wave around or force his will on it. He studies the wave, he learns to understand its nature, and he rides with it—never against it. Sometimes it is good to just ride the wave and be one with it. While uniqueness may require swimming against the current, we do not have to feel or be unique to be happy. We must be authentic, and authenticity can be found in the current.

Not everything has to be a fight and not everything has to be a conquest. We are taught to force our will on everything. To give way is considered weak. We do not live; we fight. You must win, or else you lose. There is no middle ground. It is us against nature and us against everybody else. This isolated and aggressive lifestyle and our "anti-" mentality are not conducive to happiness. We are part of nature. We are nature. Why turn against who we are?

My Will, Your Will, Our Will

I have my very own commentator in my brain. This protagonist is constantly moderating and judging my behavior, almost as if I am split in two. I know what I am supposed to do, but I either do not do it or I do it poorly. I then torment myself for falling short. As students and professionals, we rarely if ever live up to the standards we have set for ourselves, and our inner voice is constantly there to remind us of our shortcomings. Where does this voice come from? It is clearly our own—or is it?

I have long thought that I have always done what I wanted to do. I now understand that many of my decisions were not entirely based on what I truly wanted. We grow up observing adults, who often tell us what to do—our parents, our career advisors, our professors. We are raised from the outside. The voices of others and our very own voice become so comingled that it becomes difficult to discern which is which. What we perceive as our will may very well be the will seeded in us through observing, being taught, and our desire to belong. Our actions may look and feel like the product of our own will when they, in fact, grew out of seeds planted by others.

Your truth is different from my truth. My truth is different from your truth. I am not talking about absolute truth, as in that the sun is eight light minutes away, but truth in a relative sense—the truth that is relative to some particular frame of reference. In that sense, my truth and your truth are not necessarily the same.

How many times during any given day do we think what we are supposed to think instead of what we truly think according to our truth? How many times a day do we feel what we are supposed to feel instead of what we truly feel? This tendency may be particularly pronounced in the law school setting, and later in practice, where there seems to be an emphasis on conformity. The only way to experience truth clearly is to look within, to observe oneself.

Secondhand Living

In addition to our inability to discern whether what we perceive as our will is really our will, we also continue to copy the behavior we observe. We live in a secondhand environment. We observe, we ask for advice, and we do what others tell us we should do to reach a particular goal. There is nothing wrong with this; to the contrary, seeking guidance and learning from the experience of others is a natural and helpful inclination. But looking to others has the unfortunate effect of moving our sight away from ourselves. This is exacerbated by the proliferation of social media. We do not seek our own reality, but the reality promised by others. We copy, somewhat mechanically, those around us. But this can cause significant disorder. Each of us is a continuous flow of energy, moments, thoughts, and feelings. We are living and breathing organisms in a living and breathing universe. If no two humans are precisely the same, how can we think that we can find peace by copying someone else?

Since we grew up observing and being taught and directed by others, we automatically seek solutions outside of us. We do not know any other way. We live our lives thinking that the answer is out there, not in here. In addition, professional development circles encourage us to look at our shortcomings, to question ourselves. We are trained in issue spotting both within the law and within us. The only time we actually look inwards then is to find imperfection. We look outside for guidance and inside for fault. That is a terrible habit that will grow into a deep mistrust of our instincts and self-nature. How can we be great lawyers if we cannot hear our own voices and trust ourselves?

Trust Yourself

I often have received advice that made complete sense, yet something in me knew better. The proposed path or idea just did not sit right in my belly. Over the years, I have learned to listen to that elusive voice. Most of the time, it has served me well. It was usually impossible to express this feeling with words; it was vague yet crystal clear. The more I learned to listen to it, the more I gained confidence in my own compass. Even though my brain did not seem to know which path to choose, my belly always knew. This does not mean that I do not seek the counsel and wisdom of others; I always do. It is inevitable, however, that advice from multiple sources will be different and sometimes contradicting or contrary to my own voice. In these moments, I let my inner compass show me the path.

Our body has a tremendous capability to look after itself. It signals hunger, thirst, tiredness, heat, cold, danger, pleasure, and so on. In our habitual outward-looking lifestyle, though, our compass gets thrown about. Like birds in a magnetic mesh flying in a loop trying to find north, we spin in a circle trying to find truth. Our inner compass does not need any manipulation; it just needs to be left to its nature. Once freed from the bombardment of voices from outside, the needle can do what it does. She who finds trust within herself is so deeply planted that nothing can uproot her.

To not trust ourselves puts us in a rather dubious position. If we cannot trust ourselves, how can we trust our mistrusting of self? If you judge that a certain part of you is not trustworthy, how do you know that this judgment is in turn trustworthy? This ties us in a knot. On the other hand, if we trust ourselves, we trust this trust, and so on. There is no confusion. To trust ourselves is natural; to not trust ourselves is unnatural and painful and creates internal chaos.

Does this mean that we are free of faults? Is your best friend, who you trust entirely, free of faults? Of course not. She makes mistakes, but your trust has nothing to do with it. To trust ourselves does not mean that we can put our brain into sleep mode or that a mistake must destroy this trust. If we wait to trust ourselves until we feel infallible, we will never trust ourselves.

How can we be great lawyers if we cannot trust ourselves? The good judgment that outstanding attorneys develop over time is the product of experience coupled with a strong intrinsic sense of what is the right path.

We must proceed from a place of trust. Trust is the anchor that protects us from the currents of life. It is an act you can start right now, from right where you are. Try it.

7

The Opposition Culture

You vs. Me

Our culture at large glorifies individualism, embodied in the one who pulls himself up by his bootstraps and, against all odds, shapes his life to his liking. This emphasis on the individual coupled with the adversarial system in which we are taught accentuates separateness. We feel as if we are confronting life and others. The belief in distance and otherness, which is pervasive in our culture, is highlighted during our education. We are ranked among our classmates, and our rank helps determine our future position in the profession. Our minds are trained in comparison, judgment, competition, and envy. It is no wonder then that we look at life as us against them.

Me vs. Me

But it is not only us against them, it is also us against us.

When I started meditating, I was taught to focus on my breath, which I managed to do for milliseconds at a time before I wandered off. When I noticed that I had wandered, something or someone reminded me to "focus on your breath." Who was the one wandering, and who was the one calling me back? I felt schizophrenic. It was I who both wandered and who remembered the task at hand. What was supposed to be a relaxing activity made me so mad that

I was ready to let meditation be. When I heard from others how meditation changed their lives, I felt even more frustrated by my incompetence and impatience.

Just like Bruce Springsteen sings in "Two Faces," we often feel split in two. We feel at odds with ourselves. The comparing and ranking that follows us through our formal education affects how we experience what or who we are. The constant comparison of ourselves to others leads us also to compare ourselves with ourselves: what we are and what we ought to be. "Today, I was supposed to do yoga. I am so undisciplined." "Today I was hoping to finish my memo. I am not living up to my potential." What we did and what we ought to do conflicts, and here we are, one human being, divided into good and bad. How often do we feel OK with ourselves, if at all?

I am a great proponent of self-improvement. The capacity of a human being to self-reflect and regulate her behavior is a remarkable human feature, one that separates us from animals. I used to develop systems to make myself better, faster, more productive, calmer, more patient, more present, more compassionate person. Every time, I fell short of my ambitions. I found myself divided against myself more often than not: the Desiree that wanted and the Desiree that did not deliver. Confronted with a constant barrage of self-talk, I divided myself against myself. I was haunted by the sensation of a second Desiree standing over me with a club.

If we behave well, we feel satisfied that we are a good person. If we fail, we admonish ourselves for being bad. On any given day, I can do both good and bad things. I can have a lovely conversation with my dad, and a few minutes later bitch unjustifiably at a friend. Which one is me? The good or the bad? Who we are is much more complicated than good or bad—our souls cannot be forced neatly into boxes. Most of the time, we are a mixture of both good and bad at the same time. It simply does not work to squeeze a complex being like a human into neat categories. I used to get very angry with myself for being quite volatile. One day I could be in great spirits, compassionate, and caring, only to be aggressive and impatient the next. One day I could be the best student in class while the next not have one decent thought. It drove me crazy because I thought that I am either one or the other. But I am both and neither, all at once.

What does all this mean for our lives as law students and legal professionals? That inevitably we will fall short of our own assessments of what we ought to be. That we will make goals with respect to our productivity and professionalism that we will not accomplish. Does this mean that we are bad at what we do? Or is it simply a reflection of our nature as humans that we inevitably do not accomplish all of our objectives? Ideals and the perfection sought by our internal commentator are wonderful when they motivate us and force us to reflect thoughtfully. When they are a tool of punishment and remorse, they become counterproductive.

Us vs. Time

Legal education is not very long, although some might argue that it is too long. Within three years we are supposed to grow into lawyers and enter the profession.

"It's time to grow up!" is a command known to many, but we can just as easily say: "We need time to grow up." We cannot jump ahead of ourselves. Yet we attempt exactly that. There are things about us that we need to change. But at the same time, we do not need to be too desperate, too ruthless, too combative. Some things simply take time. When I was twenty-five, I was not ready for a certain kind of understanding. No matter how many times others "educated" me, I needed time to develop my own understanding. If the soil is not fertile, some things cannot take root.

While certain things take time, others require the right moment. We frustrate ourselves and we turn against ourselves if we expect too much too soon. By this, I am far from suggesting a passive approach to self-development—the mere waiting for things to get better. Development requires a certain amount of energy and dedication, but in addition it requires patience.

How can we know the right balance between the two? If we are frustrated more often than not, the scale is likely out of balance. The ever-increasing speed with which life moves puts tremendous pressure on us to grow at the same, very rapid pace. We are a society that has very little patience to allow things to unfold in their own time. But growth is a natural process that cannot be artificially accelerated without causing damage to the system. Just as a child needs time to grow up, we as adults need time for things to grow within us and to grow into things. We need time to become lawyers. We should not punish ourselves if we do not develop at the same pace as another.

Unite

So how do we reunite what has been separated over the years? If we focus on our shortcomings to the exclusion of all else, where is the root for trust? With our insistent pointing towards our imperfections, we regard ourselves more as a faulty system than a human being endowed with the tools necessary to manage life. At a minimum, we need a seed of trust from which to proceed. We need to trust that our judgment about ourselves is correct. Without this, we are lost. We need to see our shortcomings as part of a larger whole that represents us—one bad grade or imperfect negotiation does not define us.

Living in a community, of course, requires a measure of control over our instincts. But we must be careful not to be too hard on ourselves and suffocate our intuitive nature. Unfortunately, we tend to err on the side of too much control. We become mini robots. We function, but we forget how to live. To live fully, we must allow ourselves to explore every part of ourselves. A great artist is great because he allows himself to explore all corners of his personality. Control is the antidote to any artistic endeavor. While we need rules and boundaries and obviously should not follow every instinct and whim (this would go too far in the other direction), we must be all right with not being the perfect being—the perfect student, the perfect friend, the perfect husband, the perfect child. As we are encouraged to be increasingly hard on ourselves, to abhor weakness and failure, we make life mechanical. We force nature into submission; we conquer Everest and try to do the same with ourselves. We mold, squeeze, cut, dominate, and control to fit into the mold that society has chosen for us. Can we be good citizens while simultaneously living a true and perfect expression of ourselves? Can we let go of all the external expectations for ourselves and still be a compassionate neighbor, brother, and colleague? I believe that a human being is boundless, borderless, and all-encompassing. If you cut it or squeeze it, you disturb its natural tendency to expand. If we proceed as a complete whole rather than a divided house, we will get to where we want to go sooner or later. How much better can we advocate for others if we are not divided against ourselves?

Do not fight yourself, do not fight others, do not fight time. There is no need to fight. Not even in law!

8

This or That?

Law school trains us to be analytical and critical thinkers. We must be able to identify and define problems, extract key information, and develop workable solutions for the problems identified. We learn to carefully evaluate information and determine how to interpret it in order to make a sound judgment. Our thinking revolves around an "issue," a "rule," an "application," and a "conclusion" for each and every possible concern. We divide, analyze, and surmise. This way of thinking seeps into our everyday lives.

So we chunk life into having and not having, yours and mine, this and that, here and there, good and bad, successful and unsuccessful, pass and fail, guilty and not guilty, winner and loser, and so on. If something does not fit, we either cut and squeeze it to make it fit or hastily invent a new category. Once we have a new category, we are at peace again. Our urge to chunk, label, organize, and categorize focuses on life's opposites, an alternate version of 1s and 0s. But life is neither one nor zero. Life is too complex, too connected, too moving to be chopped into this or that. Life's beauty defies such classification.

Not only do we divide life into 1s and 0s, but we also want to experience only the 1s—the positives. As we divide life into boxes, we seek to eliminate the dark, the low, the ugly, and the painful. Rather than embracing the in-betweens, we seek one extreme—the supreme. But this is neither possible nor wise.

Imagine two children on the playground. As they run towards the seesaw, one child exclaims, "Let's play on the seesaw, but I only want to be up." The other child is baffled. "How do you play on the seesaw if one side is always up?" In life, we want the ups, never the downs. It is a human instinct to seek that which is good, but our society makes us believe that a happy life is a life that is *always* up. This belief is a source of frustration because there is no living soul whose life or whose emotions are always up. To seek a life full of pleasure and absent of pain is to seek a pink elephant. To chop off the uglier parts of life is to destroy its beauty, just as wanting always to be up on the seesaw destroys the fun of the game. Beauty is in the interplay between opposites. Our frustration over the challenges we face arises because we refuse to accept this.

In our quest to eliminate or avoid those memories and moments we do not like, we destroy life's beauty. Life has to be lived as a whole, not in piecemeal fashion. We cannot listen to a song by holding on to one note because we like it so much that we do not want it to disappear. By attempting to do this, we miss the entire song. A song is the flow of notes, not one note in isolation. The same is true when we try to hold on to just one instrument in a piece composed for multiple instruments. If we pick one instrument and tune out the others, the song will lose its power. You can try this experiment quickly on the internet by listening to midi files, which split the music into its component instruments. You can then mute all the instruments but one and see what happens. The song has lost its magic.

Just like a song, life is a flow of moments, not one moment in isolation. If we hold on to one moment, we miss the unfolding of the song. The note by itself has little beauty; it is what comes before and after it and how they flow together that makes the song beautiful. In life, we pick and choose and try to extract some things and tune out others. We select what is good, which we want to keep, and decide what is bad, which we want to get rid of. By doing so, we destroy the song of life. Wisdom lies in appreciating life not as an endless parade but as an interweaving of different moments that create this magical universe.

No Good Without Bad

We are a pleasure-centered society and abhor pain. Everywhere we turn, we are sold the myth that a good life is a life free of pain. The delusion we carry of a pain-free life is a result of our ever-increasing level of comfort. Groceries are delivered to the door. Our subscription to toilet paper makes it appear in steady intervals. The dishwasher cleans the dishes, the toothbrush does the spinning, the car does the parking, and our robot vacuum does the cleaning. As our comfort increases, we have a diminished ability to bear discomfort and pain. The more comfortable our life turns, the less willing we are to accept pain as a part of life.

But to be successful we must be willing to endure the pain that comes with that success. Education requires discomfort because only then will we grow. Wanting to avoid discomfort means foregoing growth, wanting to avoid pain means foregoing success. Success and pain, discomfort and growth are so connected that the further up one side of the seesaw is, the further down the other side must be. The more strength one child uses to push off the ground, the more violent her arrival will be at the top. Every great evening is followed by a painful morning. Every great love story includes heartache. Every success story includes pain. Life is a complete and perfect circle. If we try to chop the unpleasant out of that circle, we destroy the circle.

Many find the process of legal education to be grueling and the practice even more demanding. We spend a great deal of time and energy complaining about the challenges we face—everything from competitive classmates and colleagues, to demanding professors or bosses, to boredom with the more mundane aspects of the work—rather than embracing it. By attempting to live a life without its less pleasant aspects, we attempt the impossible.

Rather than striving for a life free from pain, we should strive for a life free from the fear of pain. Fearing pain is like fearing one's own breath. Freeing ourselves from the fear of pain frees us from the futile pursuit of avoiding it. A complete life is a life in which the loss of a loved one pierces your heart. This pain is what we must bear if we want to know the awesome force of love. We must choose life completely or forego it altogether. Some may choose to live a delusion if it promises a painless existence. But the shallowness of such an existence, this 2D version of life, will feel like an unending marathon. Once we free ourselves from the fear of pain, we are ready for the completeness of living. Life can be happy only when embraced, not escaped.

But Bad Without Worse

The minute we say up, there is down. The minute we say warm, there is cold. The minute we say right, there is left, and the minute we say happiness, there is pain. It does not make sense to say up when there is no down. It does not make sense to say warm when there is no cold. It does not make sense to say happiness when there is no pain. The two create each other, depend on each other, and reinforce each other. If we talk about happiness, we must speak about pain. But what about suffering?

While pain is an inescapable part of life, suffering is a response to pain—an unnecessary meta emotion. Studying for the New York bar exam was painful. I was exposed to many new subjects, such as contracts, evidence, and real estate. My master's degree was in intellectual property and information technology law and thus rather specialized. And the knowledge I had about "general" law was in a civil law system. I was not the only one in pain. Everyone in my bar prep course was equally in pain. But some were outright suffering. They tormented themselves with a constant barrage of self-talk. "I can't do this. This is too much. This is stupid. I am not going to make it. The board of law examiners are idiots. My law school did not prepare me properly." None of it had anything to do with studying for the bar exam. All of it was emotions and chatter that was added to the task at hand: studying. Studying ten hours a day was painful, but suffering I was not. I kept my mouth shut and took care of what needed to be done.

To live life fully, we must experience pain. But a full life does not necessitate suffering. Some may not see a difference between the two because suffering follows their pain like the cart follows the horse. They do not or are unwilling to recognize that one can detach the cart and just ride the horse. Suffering is a choice; pain is not.

Sugar and Salt

I am not the person you want to have in your kitchen. Whatever I do in the kitchen always results in a mess. For some reason, gravity seems strongest in the kitchen. I spend more time wiping things off the floor than preparing food. During Christmas one year, I made cookies with my nieces and nephews. I cannot recall ever making cookies before, so I was quite excited. My niece was tasked with giving instructions, and we were assigned to follow them. "Desiree," she said, "get the salt!" "What do you need salt for?" I asked. "For the cookie dough," she replied. "That can't be right," I thought and took the recipe from her. "Look at that; it calls for salt." It turns out that salt is an essential ingredient as it heightens the flavor of all other ingredients, even sweets. One would only taste salt if we either used too much or did not mix the batter properly. Sweet and salty are opposites, yet a great cookie requires the balancing of both.

Contrast, the difference in brightness between objects, is a critical element in photography. Just as a good photograph has the right contrast, just like a cookie has the right mix of sugar and salt, a good life requires contrast. When I spend a few days in silent meditation, consuming only rice, beans, and water, I cannot wait for the first bite of French fries. Those fries taste better than any others I had before, but they, too, soon will lose their appeal.

When I spend an entire day in the office, I cannot wait to take a walk. When I spend a day walking through the city, I cannot wait to finally sit in my office. The contrasting nature of our experience is what makes life rich. Our comfort society largely eliminates this contrast so that things, events, hours, and days blend into each other. By eliminating inconveniences and struggle, we eliminate life's contrast.

We have a saying in German: "Dir geht es wohl zu gut." This can be translated loosely as "It looks like you are too comfortable." We would say this in response to someone who comes up with an idiotic idea. Only someone who is too comfortable can make a stupid suggestion in an attempt to spice things up. This implies that if we are too comfortable, we tend to push the envelope to build contrast.

In the same vein, we often invent problems where there are none. We turn inconveniences into problems, disagreements into fights. My best friend recently complained about her coffee machine breaking just when she was about to make coffee. She was beside herself with anger. Her reaction was utterly disproportionate to a broken coffee machine simply because she is too comfortable. She artificially created contrast.

Our path to becoming well rounded legal professionals requires a pinch of salt here and there. It is a necessary ingredient. We need to leave the edges and roughness in our lives. Nature is not polished; it is rough. The more we try to smooth life, the more unnatural we make it, and the blander it becomes. We should embrace the corners, the edges, and the roughness in our lives and appreciate life's contrasts. The salty moments in life are those that heighten the flavor of everything else. A two-hour evidence class will make the beer you have with your friends afterwards taste so much better.

The In-Between

If there are not two sides to a coin then there is no coin, because the coin is in-between two sides. In the same vein, if we eliminate the in-between, we eliminate the essence of life. Happiness is found in the in-between.

The minute I started studying law in Germany I could not wait to graduate. The minute I started my first internship, I could not wait for it to be over. The minute I started my LLM, I could not wait to move on to the bar exam. Whenever I started a new adventure, I was elated for the first few days, only to look ahead to the elation that would come at the conclusion. Each year during orientation week, I remind my students that in the whirlwind of the coming months, they should not forget to pause and enjoy the experience. Yes, law school can be enjoyed; it must be enjoyed. Starting law school and graduating from law school are milestones, but it is the time in between these milestones that is the most precious. It is in this time that we evolve, that we grow, that we become, that we live. Graduation marks the end of this cycle and the beginning of a new cycle. When we find our first job as a junior associate, we kick off a new cycle that must be lived, embraced, and enjoyed.

I like devices, even the most unnecessary ones, such as the scale that connects to my phone and the toothbrush that tells me where to brush. Whenever there is something new on the market, I feel the urge to own it.

Whenever I buy something that I want, I am elated for the first days. I handle the new device with much care. I look at it and enjoy the excitement that it brings me. The moments before complete possession takes place are the most exciting ones—the moment between wanting and owning. I go to the store, pick up the item, pay, walk home while looking at the box, open the door, make myself a coffee, and get comfortable on the sofa. I look at the box, move it in my hands, caress it, and start opening it very slowly. I investigate how it is packaged. I take the device in my hand as carefully as I can. I inspect it for scratches and other imperfections. I have it right here in my hand, but it is not yet fully mine. Even when the device is unwrapped, turned on, and used, it is still not entirely mine. It still feels foreign, new, and it will take some time to fully own it. But once I claim complete ownership, the excitement slowly fades, and the new device becomes just another thing I possess. It is the moment between wanting and not yet fully having that is the most exciting. Neither the moments of not having nor the moments of having can provide the same emotion as the moment between the two. We see the same phenomenon when we watch children play on a seesaw; it is the moment between the top and the bottom, the transition from high to low, that provides the most joy.

In our contemporary life, the in-betweens get increasingly obscured. The time between wanting and having diminishes rapidly. Whatever we seek, we shall get, expedited and delivered to the door. Going from wanting to having in ever shorter periods, we cut out the in-between that makes life exciting.

We must not look at life as a collection of this and that, where "this" must be sought and "that" must be avoided. For something to have an in-between, it must have two sides, and there is no one side without the other.

9

Not Every Itch
Must Be Scratched

Any mention of freedom provokes thoughts of political freedom—freedom from persecution and from discrimination. But freedom presents another contemporary dilemma: self-made shackles.

I knew from the time I was about twelve years old that I was gay, but it was not yet common to be open, especially in the little German village in which I was living. I never heard of anyone being with a same-sex partner. I had no terms with which to define myself. All I knew was that something was not the way it was supposed to be. So I lied to myself and became so accustomed to lying that I trapped myself in my own deceit. Deceit was all I knew, and I could not escape. Even when society became more open to homosexuality, I was stuck in the comfort of what I knew best—lying.

I did not know any life other than the one in which my true self was forced to hide. Until I was thirty years old, I knew nothing of the freedom of embracing my partner in public or saying "girlfriend." Until then, my every thought and action were carefully crafted theater performances. I lived in a self-made prison. And the longer I lived in it, the more impenetrable the prison walls seemed. Had I known that the doors were wide open all along and that all I needed to do was to step out, I would have done it ten years earlier.

When I came out to my father at age thirty, I did not even have the courage to call him, so I texted him instead. He phoned me immediately, and I was terrified to pick up because I was afraid of losing his love. When I picked up the phone, he was laughing and said, "Sweetheart, I always knew, but it wasn't my place to tell you. I needed to wait until you were ready to stand for who you are." After that, I told the rest of my family, and with every person who knew, I could breathe a little easier. Now, living my life completely in the open, I cannot imagine how I functioned within my fake life. Through my very own choices, I surrendered my freedom.

Freedom from Passions

One does not need to hide one's sexuality to find oneself in chains. Our commercialist society and our desire for power and money fill us with wants and needs that bind us. Society creates a mirage to which we fall prey. How many of us started law school to fight injustice only to end up doing M&A transactions? Part of what moves us from our goals is the crushing amount of debt we have, but we also do many things because we follow imaginary promises to meet imaginary needs. We bind ourselves by needing the wanted and attempting to avoid the unwanted. Our contemporary problem is not lacking but seeking.

I used to consider my ability to follow my passions a measure of my freedom. If I have the means to do what I really want to do, then I am free. I am grateful that I now live a life in which I am free to follow my passions, yet I do not feel the freedom that I expected. On the contrary, sometimes, I feel quite trapped.

"Follow your passion" has become a buzz phrase used by self-help gurus, and to find one's passion is considered the path to happiness. But to follow our passions is to tie ourselves to them, and not every passion is worth being bound to. Happiness does not require us to follow every passion. On the contrary, following every passion can be outright detrimental to happiness.

The word passion comes from the Latin *passionem*, meaning suffering or enduring. It is sometimes described as the state of being affected by or acted upon by external forces. Many passions are reactions to stimuli from our environment. We are, in the truest sense, acted upon. If we blindly react to passions, we become like Pavlov's dog.

Law school or legal practice can feel suffocating. But we are not suffocated by law school or practice. Instead, we are suffocated by all the things society tells us we should be owning, doing, and being. As lawyers, we are acted upon incessantly. Do we want to work in Big Law because that is what we really want, or is there a sense of pride inbeing able to secure such a job? Do we want to make partner because that is our calling or because that is the badge of accomplishment for which others strive and for which others will value us?

It is difficult to see the connection between our passions and our lack of freedom because we are conditioned to believe that happiness and freedom require the ability to scratch every itch. How can freedom possibly be reconciled with passion—"the state of being affected by?" By what are we affected if we are free? I do not want to be the dog that starts salivating when the metronome begins clicking.

To be free from blind reactive passions, we need discipline. We are prone to think that discipline restricts our freedom, but discipline is the required structure within which freedom can unfold. Discipline assists us in freeing ourselves from blind passions. Discipline allows us to detach the strings that make us move like puppets. If we have the discipline to forego, the discipline to discern, the discipline to defend, the discipline to listen to our true nature, then we can be truly free.

Law school teaches us the necessary discipline. It is this very rigor that can prevent us from being pushed around by blind passions.

Whim

I am incredibly impatient; I would rather pay more for something and get it in store than buy it cheaper online and wait. Delayed gratification is foreign to me.

Our prosperity opens increased possibilities. We do not lack opportunities but are suffocated by them. The number of options can easily be overwhelming if we design our lives based on impulses. Indeed, many of our so-called passions may be reduced to mere whims. Law school and practice can easily become overwhelming when we do not decline to follow whims.

A whim is a desire that emerges suddenly. And since we believe that a good life is based on fulfilling our every desire, we seek to fulfill whims. But a whim is a desire unlike others. Alan Watts says that "[a] whim responds to the question, 'Why not?' as opposed to the question 'Why?'"

Which question is more conducive to a happy life: "Why?" or "Why not?" When I asked my friends this question, they almost unanimously answered, "Why not?" They explained that "Why not?" exhibits a certain zest for life and an openness to possibilities. I was wondering how much of their answer was due to our social and cultural conditioning. Our culture teaches us that we should step outside our comfort zone, try new things, and not shy away from experiences. I agree with this advice. However, there is a difference between choosing an experience because we have an innate motivation for it and choosing an experience because we cannot find a reason against it. To guide our life with the question "Why not?" is very different from a much more purposeful life driven by "Why?"

We are faced with a multitude of opportunities through which we can develop our careers: networking events, lectures, panel discussions, webinars, seminars, bootcamps. We try to take in as much as we can. When we decide to participate, we often do so because we asked ourselves "Why not?" as opposed to "Why?" After all, it cannot hurt to go to the event on space law. So, why not?

If we structure our day based on "Why not?" we will be burned out before we reach age thirty. Just because we can do many things for our career does not mean that we should be doing all of them. We can passively accept every invite, or we can actively choose something we genuinely want. Only the latter is living.

Living life by choosing things or activities based on whether there are reasons against it can make life cluttered and complicated. Wanting something because we have reasons for it is living life; doing something because we cannot find a reason to say "no" is being lived. Just because we can do something does not mean that we should. With the freedom to choose comes the responsibility to select. Freedom means being able to choose opportunities based on internal motivation. Confusing this freedom with the freedom to do everything is to slowly become shackled by life.

Freedom from Choice

About once a month, I participate in a virtual mediation retreat. My days are highly structured, starting at five in the morning. I set up strict rules for myself during these retreats. Every choice that I have during a "normal" day is taken away. The type and amount of food I consume is set, my schedule is set, my activities are set (walking, sitting, cleaning the house). The only real choice that I am left with is whether to stick to these rules. I choose to spend a week without having choices—I choose to be free from choice. To some, this may look like a too austere way of being. Why would a person with all the conveniences of the twenty-first century choose to eat one bowl of rice and beans a day and stare at a wall for fourteen hours?

But the rules that I set provide the foundation for the unfolding of freedom. It is precisely because I have no choices that I am free to just be. There are no questions in my head, no balancing between this and that. After every meditation retreat, I struggle to get back to "normal" life. At first, I am excited about watching TV, having dinner with my wife, and being in touch with my family. But this is accompanied by a feeling of loss—the loss of simplicity that freed me from the responsibility of having to make decisions. Such an austere life is neither sustainable, nor is it the kind of life I would want, but it reminds me every time anew that choice does not always equate with freedom.

When we are in law school, we long to get out—to be free of it. Law school seems to restrict our current choices because we have to study and perform according to a schedule set by others. When I studied for the bar exam I longed for the day when I could do what I want. My days were highly structured, and, except for the occasional dinner, I had no time to play with. But instead of feeling free after the bar exam, I felt lost. I woke up the morning after and had no idea what to do with myself. I could go for a walk, to the gym, for breakfast, meet a friend, call my mom, read a book, watch TV…. I felt paralyzed by all the things I could be doing. In an ironic twist, I missed the "prison" of bar prep for quite some time after.

Yet we often equate having choices with freedom. When you limit my choices, you restrict my freedom. That is why we want more money. We assume that when we are rich and have lots of money, we can do and buy whatever we want and that this will give us a sense of greater freedom. But we can still feel a lack of freedom even amidst infinite resources and choices. Most of the powerful and wealthy that I know have ulcers and acid reflux and are chased by their phones like a horse by a whip. The castle they have built is the prison that suffocates them. More choices do not lead to freedom.

With choice comes an enormous amount of responsibility and anxiety. We do not just want to make the right choices; we strive to make the best choices. Because we can never be sure whether a choice is indeed the best, every choice leaves us insecure. Every semester when our post-graduate students register for classes, I see the terror that choices bring. Students can choose from hundreds of courses. They are not anxious because of a lack of opportunity but because they are overwhelmed by options.

In my everyday life, I start to cut away choices by disciplining myself. Rather than asking, "Will I write today?" I discipline myself to write one thousand words every single day. There is no choice. Likewise, I discipline myself to meditate every day for one hour at 7:00 am and one hour at 7:00 pm. The first days were difficult because there was still some residue of choice: "Should I really do this?" "Is this too much?" But once I had decided and eliminated the choice, it became the easiest thing to do. There is no "if," "when," or "where." There is no choice between sleeping an extra hour or sitting on the cushion. And as bizarre as it may sound, the more discipline I exert, the freer I feel. I guard my discipline because it is my gateway to freedom. It is my discipline that frees me from the currents of constant temptation, seductions, and promises.

Freedom from Impression

I remember the first week of law school in the U.S. The Socratic method was new to me and the idea of having to speak in front of the entire class with my German accent terrified me. The more terrified you look, the faster you will be called upon, and so very early in the semester I was called to answer a question that involved a gerbil. I had never heard of the word gerbil before so I stared rather dumbfounded at my professor while the class stared, puzzled, at me. I was very well aware of the impression I had just made.

In law school we seek to impress the professor and outshine our peers; in practice we seek to impress the partners and outshine our colleagues. But it unfortunately does not stop there. Never has there been a time when being in the public eye was as important as it is today. Our most mundane activities, such as eating lunch, are broadcast into the world. Humans have always been concerned with the impressions they make. Today's technology exacerbates this concern a thousandfold. Our social media accounts require a consistent stream of pictures and tag lines. Our days revolve around the digital impressions that we make and the feedback—likes and shares—that we receive. Bruce Lee said that "[f]reedom discovers man the moment he loses concern over what impression he is making or about to make." If Bruce Lee is right, we are far from free.

I am quite shy, and being in a group of people or meeting someone for the first time was a struggle for many years. I was often paralyzed by my concern over the impression that I was making. I choreographed and watched my body movements, how I sat, how I held my arms, what I said, and the way I said it. I was always exhausted afterward and had the strength only for a few such meetings in any given month. People around me did not notice it and often assumed that I was quite comfortable in public. They thought so because that is precisely the impression that I wanted them to have. They fell prey to my act. Today, I do not have any social media accounts other than LinkedIn because I simply want to be free from the need to impress. Through a painstaking chipping away, I am slowly freeing myself from the concern over what impression I am making. The few instances in which I get to glimpse into a life free of such concerns make me want to pursue this freedom with all my might.

Freedom from the Tyranny of the Majority

In addition to being concerned with impressing others, we constantly absorb the content and messaging of others, mainly through social media. I deliberately do not follow any social media accounts, nor do I have cable television. When I am constantly bombarded by the voices of others, it is much more difficult to hear my own. Everywhere we turn, we hear words and see images. The very first thing most of us do when we wake up is to grab our phones. Before the brain has fully awakened, we are already impressed upon by content. We are addicted to it. We absorb everyone's world and completely neglect our own. Where is the silence?

When I was twenty-one years old, I moved from a small town to a larger city in Germany. Within a few months, I adopted the local intonation. The rise and fall of my voice morphed into the rise and fall of the voices around me. My family laughed about the way I spoke, which, of course, I did not even notice. We copy what others do and what they value. Freedom is not freedom if it is merely the freedom to act like everybody else. As Nietzsche said, we are flattening mountains and valleys. In an ironic twist, our very striving for uniqueness makes us fall prey to herd mentality. On social media and elsewhere, we are quite literally following others. How can following be equated with freedom?

True freedom is freedom from whims and passions and from the concern over the impression we are making. True freedom is being guided by our own voice rather than the noise of the majority. The discipline we acquire as lawyers can help us free ourselves from whims, passions, impressions, and the tyranny of the majority.

10

Embrace the Ordinary

Life, at its most fundamental level, is simple. We are born, we die, and in between we eat, sleep, and perform other essential bodily functions. Leaving aside the complexity of our organism, on the surface, this is all there is to it. Since life is naturally simple, it would make sense to strive for the ordinary and simple. Yet we move, consciously or unconsciously, toward complexity. We race on the hedonic treadmill and then become dissatisfied with the superficiality of our existence. We look for solutions in the desire for more, and we run away from emptiness and non-activity. By doing so, just like the universe at large, our lives hurdle towards entropy.

For scientists, simplicity is the guide to truth. The physicist Richard Feynman noted that "[t]he truth always turns out to be simpler than you thought." Then, there is Occam's razor, the law of parsimony, which states that entities should not be multiplied needlessly. I long disregarded this simple truth and added to my possessions—objects, titles, degrees, medals—hoping that each addition would bring happiness. In my attempt to live a happy life, I made life ever more complicated.

Shortly after I started writing this book, I made a vow to focus on simplicity. I vowed to notice when things are unnecessarily complicated and to evaluate what is indeed needed and what is a well-trained reaction to commercialism. This task turned out to be more challenging than I thought. I cannot distinguish what is necessary from that which is a mere convenience or, worse, unnecessary. I continue to fool myself into believing that something superfluous is indeed necessary.

In line with my simplicity vow, I imagined spending time in a car, driving across the country, eating beans out of a can, and sitting under the sky. I could not imagine anything simpler. After my imagination crafted the most uncomplicated version of travel it could fathom, my spoiled and comfort-seeking Western mind kicked in and started adding "necessities." Sleeping in a car without a toilet? What if I have to pee in the middle of the night? Maybe instead of a car, I should rent a little camper van. So I started researching camper vans, and it was such a pleasure to see what "necessities" one can squeeze into a little truck. One can have a wet bath, a plug-in stove, and a fan. It turns out that it is quite expensive to rent such a van. So I thought since my life will be more straightforward from now on and since I will travel like this more in the future, perhaps I should buy one! So, off I went to the camper store. I ended up purchasing a Class B RV with a full bathroom, shower, stove, fridge, oven, microwave, air conditioning, and solar panels.

After I purchased the RV, I started to learn more about what is required to maintain it. Where does the electricity come from? Where does water come from and go to? What about toilet waste? How do I protect the pipes from freezing in the winter? Where do I store it? How do I keep rodents from biting through the wires and pipes and living in my RV? My research produced a full-blown panic attack. Instead of simplicity, I added an enormous headache to my life. The camper store was kind enough to cancel my RV order. Once I was relieved of the device that was to make my travel simpler, I could breathe again. What had just happened? How could my vow of simplicity have led me so far astray?

Months have passed since I vowed to make my life simpler. Although my life looks much the same, my awareness of what is truly necessary has changed dramatically. I live with all the conveniences one can imagine, and I have more than I could ever ask for. But I recognize now that addition is an addiction of our society and a distortion of human needs.

The Tools of Tools

Many modern tools are designed to simplify our lives, and apps and professional development tools are among those we know best. At my peak, I had an app for everything except for keeping track of my bowel movements (although I recently discovered that there is indeed an app called "poop tracker"). When I was more bitchy than usual, I immediately opened my health app to see if this could be explained by my menstrual cycle. I was bitchy before I opened the app and after I closed the app, so it escapes me how this app really enriched my life.

The other day I went for a walk and discovered five minutes into my walk that I left my phone at home. I was not too concerned that I could not be reached, but I was quite distressed about the fact that my step tracker would be off. "I am not getting any credit for this walk," I thought. I considered returning home. The absurdity of my "predicament" hit me like a sledgehammer. My body walks and knows that it is walking without an app tracking it. I make myself crazy trying to reach 10,000 steps, a number calculated somewhat randomly. Rather than appreciating the sun or the trees that lined my path, I was distressed about having forgotten my phone. When I returned home, in a fit of anger about my perverted priorities, I deleted each and every app from my phone except for email and WhatsApp. I pee when I need to pee, I drink when I am thirsty, I eat when I am hungry, and I sleep when I am tired. Life really does not get simpler than that. So why do we feel the need to have apps and tools to simplify life? Because we are told that life is difficult and a struggle unless we have the right tools to manage it.

Thoreau writes in *Walden* that "[m]en become the tools of their tools." With an array of apps and digital tools to make us more efficient, more productive, healthier, and calmer, one might ask, who is really the tool? We have an app that reminds us to drink, an app that reminds us to breathe, an app that reminds us to move, an app that reminds us to put the phone aside, an app that counts our macronutrients, an app that counts our steps, an app that tells us when to go to bed, a device that reminds us to sit upright, and so forth. On the professional side, we have study tools, professional development tools, productivity tools, networking tools, and so on.

Tools that are meant to simplify our lives complicate the natural and the simple. By relying more and more on our tools, we forget how to respond to the world naturally. Our tools do not cure problems; they mask them. If we are too busy in our lives to notice when we are dehydrated, no application in the world will do us any good. Dehydration is the side effect; the problem is being too busy. When we do not know how to build and nurture relationships, no networking tool in the world will help us. Tools will paralyze us, and we will become unable to listen to the most fundamental of human needs if they are not managed carefully.

All This Stuff

Before moving to the United States, I lived in Cologne, Germany, for about ten years. I accumulated a lot of stuff along the way—things I needed, or so I thought. When I decided to move to the U.S., I had to think about these things in a different light. What should I do with them? Bring them? Too expensive! Throw them away? Too important! Store them? Where?

After deciding to store most of my possessions in my mother's cellar and bring only what I needed for the first months in the U.S., I had to decide what to store and what to bring. There were the obvious items that needed to come with me—passport, birth certificate, laptop, phone, charger, toothbrush, and clothes—but that is where the trouble started. I could not possibly bring all the clothes I owned, even though I thought I possessed very little. So I sorted through my clothing and decided on a few items to bring. Some of the rest were donated; others went into boxes to be stored. Now that I had separated out my "necessities," what about all the rest? I grabbed a few books that were important to me, a few framed photos, some gifts that I received over the years, a fountain pen, a few pieces of cheap jewelry, perfume, my bed linens, and that was it. It was a random collection of items, and not much thinking went into my choices. Everything else went into boxes with equally little consideration. After a few weeks of work, much of what I had thought of as representing my life was wrapped up and delivered to my mom's cellar, leaving me with two and a half suitcases. Because of the necessity of the task, it felt neither frightening nor sad. I did what was necessary to follow my dream to the U.S. If it meant that I had to shed my feathers, so be it. The boxes have been in my mom's cellar for more than nine years, and I have not opened them once. How much did I really need those things?

When students come into my office, it usually takes a few minutes for them to control their belongings. They are holding their phone, a computer, a book, a notebook, a pen, a Starbucks coffee, a Cava salad, and a bag, all the while headphones are dangling around their neck. Once they untangle themselves and finally sit down, they take a sip of their Frappuccino and ask: "Can you suggest a tool for handling my stress better?" "How about getting rid of about eighty percent of the things you are carrying around?" I ask. "What do you mean? What does that have to do with stress? I need all this," is the usual reply. We tend to have a somewhat skewed view about what we truly need. When we are stressed, it does not occur to us that it is because we have too much; we assume it is because we have too little.

A childhood experience first taught me that more is not necessarily better. I have a somewhat weird condition in which blisters form under the soles of my feet for no apparent reason. These are not tiny blisters but giant, painful blisters that make it impossible to walk or even wear shoes. The first time they appeared was when, as a child, I visited my grandparents in Naples, Italy. My grandmother suggested that she poke them open so that I could walk again. The thought of a needle approaching these painful blisters was outlandish. I thought it made much more sense to add cream and bandages. We argued about this, and I thought I had won.

One night while I slept, my grandmother came into my room with a freshly sanitized needle and opened all of my blisters. When I woke up in the morning, I was outraged. I felt so betrayed by the grandmother I loved so much. How could she do this to me? I refused to speak to her for what felt like days but probably was only about five minutes. Was I angry about her forever tainting my sleep with an image of her standing over me with a needle? Or was I mad because she took the pain away from me with such a simple remedy? I wanted to add cream and bandages, but a poke with a needle was a much better salve from pain. Nothing I could have added would have had the same result.

"When I have my house, my family, my car, and my beach place, then I will be happy." This is the same as saying, "I cannot be happy now because I lack a house, a family, a car, and a beach place," and that only the addition of these things will bring about happiness. Many of us view unhappiness as the result of lacking something, the addition of which will make us feel better. Therefore, we start adding education, degrees, titles, power, prestige, money, stuff, friends, connections, followers, likes, shares, experiences, and so on. After each addition, the emptiness is at least as profound as it was before. But rather than stopping to think about this, we just keep adding on the assumption that we have not yet added enough or that we have added the wrong things. We believe that our cure to unhappiness is "more."

But if "more" is the path to happiness, then the few remaining remote primitive tribes in the world must be miserable. Compared to our materialistic existence, they have close to nothing. Yet evidence suggests that they are at least as happy as we are. On a rational level, we may all understand this fact, yet we fall prey to the *more* dogma in our everyday life. In our attempt to fit in, we follow each other on the hedonic treadmill hoping that others know more than we do. The 24/7 media cycle adds to this. Businesses need to sell, so they make us believe that we need to buy. I very much enjoy the comforts of modern life, but I do not want to be its slave. The *Dao de Ching* instructs: "Instead of pouring in more, better stop while you can." By subtracting rather than adding, one can be freed. We are so focused on adding that we miss the pathway of reducing, of cutting away. When it comes to happiness, we must cut, we must reduce.

All These Titles

I recently had a conversation with my boss about changing my title from "Director of International Programs" to "Director of Global Engagement and International Programs." Does the latter version not sound more impressive? After wasting my own and everyone else's time, I got what I wanted; my title is now longer, but my life remains exactly the same.

Summer associate, junior associate, senior associate, partner, non-equity partner, equity partner, of-counsel—our profession is one of titles and our title communicates our place in the system. But does our focus on tiles add to or complicate our lives?

Our self-worth in life is closely connected to the titles we carry, or so we think. We live our lives as if we need to justify our very existence. We have to earn our place in life. "I am an Attorney, a *Diplom Jurist*, a Weightlifter, a Marathon Runner, an Author." "She accomplished nothing in her life!" is one of the most painful verdicts. Who is the judge? And what are considered accomplishments? I like to think that I am the judge of whether my time on this earth is well spent, but it is often the judgment of the people around me that makes me move in one or the other direction. I pride myself on my individualism, but I am a puppet with a fetish for titles.

I have evidence of my accomplishments on my wall: My law degrees, my certificates of admission to the bars of New York and the Supreme Court of the United States, adorned with pictures of me alongside Chief Justice Roberts and Justice Ginsberg. Next to it are my marathon, Spartan race, and weightlifting medals, which are alongside my movie poster and CD cover, right behind my coffee mug with a picture of the cover of my first book. Here are my achievements; here is a life that proved its worth. I forgot one crucial detail in the quest for all of these, *having* does not do much; *being* is the key—being not as in "I am an attorney," but being as in "I am."

I wanted to publish a book, and the act of researching, learning, thinking, and writing gives me much joy. However, if I wanted to publish a book so it looks good on my resume or spruces up my LinkedIn profile, what a torturous activity writing would become. I have been there. I wanted to be an actress to be famous, not for the craft. As a result, acting classes and training were horrendous experiences. There is no value in the number of accomplishments, only in the quality of the pursuit. When we jump from achievement to achievement, we miss the life that is in between these goals. Achievement is an end; moving towards it is living.

A happy life does not demand the adding up of accomplishments. We are happy when we see, feel, and hear—when we live. Accomplishing marks an end, the realization of a possibility. Happiness is in living, not in an end. A happy life is a life that is lived, not a life in which our main concern is collecting.

Education sets us up on the path to accomplishments and nourishes our thirst for achievement. Striving and working for something can be part and parcel of a happy life. However, if we are pursuing achievement in the belief that it will secure happiness, we are on the wrong path. The achievement will do nothing for our happiness, but the road to achievement might if it is based on intrinsic motivation.

Sweet Emptiness

In our society, emptiness has a negative connotation and is to be avoided. If we feel empty, we seek that which can fill the cavity—money, power, things, love, prestige, honor, you name it. Time in our schedule needs to be filled, even if it is just by looking at

Instagram. So much of my life thus far has been a fight against emptiness. When taking a break from work or studies, we rarely just *are*. Instead, we fill time with tasks that neither are important nor contribute to our wellbeing.

While studying the world's religions over the years, I was never particularly drawn to Buddhism. Words like "emptiness" and "void" sent shivers down my spine, and on that superficial basis, I decided that Buddhism was not for me. I rejected Buddhism because I rejected the notion of "emptiness." I received my first book on Buddhism sometime in my early twenties. The first time I actually dared to approach it seriously was when I started writing this book, some twenty years later. Now, my relationship with emptiness has changed.

How useful is a cup that does not have a cavity to hold our coffee? How useful is an apartment that has so much stuff inside that one cannot enter? How useful is a car that does not have space for a driver and passengers? A cup requires emptiness to be a cup, an apartment requires emptiness to be an apartment, and a car needs emptiness to be a car. Does a human require emptiness to be human?

What do we actually mean when we say that we feel empty? Leaving aside serious mental illness, our everyday feelings of emptiness result from mental clutter—a mind muddled with thoughts, fears, anger, stress, worries, and responsibilities. Just like a sponge that is completely filled cannot receive any more liquid, a human whose mind is too cluttered cannot take in life. We feel empty because we are too full.

Students often ask me for book recommendations or events they should attend, something that they can learn to help them manage stress and anxiety. I hesitate to recommend anything other than unplugging. We are already brimful of content from various sources, and adding will not bring about the relief we seek.

Life is inside of us. The outside world just provides the stimulus. But if our inside is filled up to the brim, where is room for life to enter? We think of an empty heart as something sad. But only an empty heart can be receptive and open to beauty and love. We need to leave enough emptiness in our hearts and in our minds for life to enter, to be able to grasp the vastness and magic of our universe. If we do not leave enough room, only a fraction of life can enter, making life seem rather unexceptional.

If we perceive emptiness as a lack of something, we view it in the negative. But what if we were to perceive emptiness as the "state of being able to receive?" A cup can be seen as either lacking content or ready to be filled. A trunk can be seen as empty or ready to be loaded. By the same token, we can regard emptiness as a lack of something or the ability to receive.

Rather than seeking to fill emptiness, we should honor emptiness as a necessary condition for happiness. A mind must be empty of judgment, stress, anger, fear, and worry to be able to see life. Rather than trying to fill our lives and minds, we should embrace emptiness.

Non-Doing

When students are stressed, they ask me what they can do. When I answer "nothing," they look perplexed. "Do nothing," I tell them. "Just stop running around like your pants are on fire." Rather than focusing on what more we could do, it makes more sense to look at how non-doing can benefit us.

Lawyers and law students barely have a second in their day during which they are doing nothing. Doing nothing feels terribly wrong because we live in a culture that glorifies and rewards activity. Even if we lie on the sofa, we either stare into our phones, watch TV, or read a book. That is not nothing. During quarantine, I realized that there was not a second in the day when I was not doing something. I woke up and grabbed my phone. While brushing my teeth, I checked the news. I talked on the phone and answered emails while having breakfast. I listened to a podcast while walking. I read a book while having the TV on. And to round out the day, I had the TV on the entire night because I cannot sleep without it. Not only am I never truly not doing anything, but I am doing multiple things at the same time. Brushing my teeth becomes so dull that I need to stimulate my addicted mind with news while spitting into the sink.

Even though I was frantically "doing," I was bored. And the more bored I became, the more I added. Dumbfounded and frustrated, I started to strip away. TV in the night, gone. Instagram, gone. News alerts, gone. I also began to focus on doing one activity at a time—I would just sit, just walk, or just eat, and do it thoroughly and wholeheartedly. This was not easy. When I ate, I instinctively took my phone to check or write a message or take a picture of my meal. It has been months since I started emptying my day and "adding" non-doing. I struggle with it tremendously. I am so addicted to the constant bombardment of stimuli that I seem unable to not-do.

My effort of non-doing showed me how easily I let time be taken away from me. Every day, I have to make a conscious effort to safeguard my time and make space for non-doing. It is not only people that I allow to intrude into my space; I also allow situations to unravel so that they take over my time. A simple task such as paying a bill turns into a prolonged period of resetting the password, calling customer service, and verifying my identity with an endless assault of codes. An activity that I "squeezed" in while writing turned out to completely control the afternoon. A quick drink with a friend ends three hours later. A quick question by a coworker turns into a forty-five-minute conversation. If I am not alert, an entire week will have passed, with me having little memory of where the time went. At the end of the week, I will feel unsatisfied and beaten in my race against time.

What good does it do to have moments of non-doing? How is this conducive to happiness? If we are too occupied to actually live anything fully, we end up in bed at night wondering where the day went. Even though we were busy, we feel as if we have done nothing. Inactivity is necessary to notice and to feel.

Please Don't Tell Me That I Am Ordinary

For my entire life, I have sought to discover and confirm my specialness. The thought of being an average person depressed me deeply. In all my pursuits, I sought not only recognition and a reason for my existence but also proof that I was indeed special. We brag, we exaggerate, we emphasize, we filter—we do just about anything we can to receive some recognition of our uniqueness. We have a difficult time accepting that, like most people, we are quite average. Why do we seek confirmation of our specialness, of our uniqueness? Why is being ordinary so difficult to accept?

Being average is a big problem in the world of competition in which we find ourselves as law students and lawyers. We are ranked among our peers, and their gain is our loss. Being average just does not cut it. We must be ranked at the top of our class.

We like to be distinguishable from other people so that we can feel our identity. If we are merely average, we blend in and lose ourselves in the crowd. This is especially true if we are in an environment of many similar beings, such as a law school or a big city. The more people there are in our close vicinity, the more we battle to feel our distinctiveness. The only way we know how to feel that we exist as a distinct being for a distinct reason with a distinct purpose is to make ourselves stand out from the crowd. We do this by seeking to be exceptional—in our grades or class ranking, our job, our wealth, our skills, our intelligence, and our talent. This inclination is exacerbated by social media and self-help protocols. We are encouraged to embrace and celebrate uniqueness. We glorify nonconformity and unconventionality. If I say to my friend that she is squarely average, she would be insulted. But this race for specialness can cause great mental chaos because it collides with our everyday experience.

We work to secure food and shelter and do fun things in between. We love our family and friends. We are pretty simple. What is wrong with it? By giving specialness more value than averageness, we end up feeling worthless and battle for what is statistically unattainable.

Even if we could be that exceptional someone who discovers the theory of relativity and changes the way humankind understands the universe forever, in the final minute of our last day we will face the same ultimate fate as everyone else. Since there is no special-ness in death, why do we think there must be specialness in life?

If we can make peace with our averageness, we can simplify our lives tremendously. Most of us probably are average with respect to most qualities. Feeling and accepting our averageness is a measure of self-awareness, which is far better than delusion. How simple our lives would be if we could rid ourselves of the burden of specialness.

Hannah Hrabarska, a Ukrainian news photographer, found liberating the revelations in *Sapiens* by Yuval Noah Harari, that she was only "one of the billions and billions that lived, and didn't make any impact and didn't leave any trace." Hrabarska said, "you kind of relax, don't feel this pressure anymore—it's O.K. to be insignificant."

Silence

Silence is the simplest of sounds, yet it is the hardest to bear. You do not have to live in New York City to be bombarded with noise. I use noise here in the broadest of meanings—noise includes not only audible stimuli but also the written word, the sung or spo-ken word, and the painted message. Few areas in our daily life are devoid of noise. We are swimming in a sea of messages, pulling us in every direction.

We have a 24/7 news cycle. How much news is there to report on any given day? Even at the height of the pandemic, there was only so much news to report. Everything else was noise. Add social media into the mix, and we have an outright assault on silence. How can we find our voice amidst this bombardment? This mental assault on our equanimity is an assault on our inde-pendence, as well.

We run away from silence because once it is there, we come face to face with ourselves. We use outside noise to obscure the path inward. But we should not run away from silence. On the contrary, we should move towards it. For in silence lies all there is for us to know. We should not think of silence as the lack of sound; we instead should think of silence as the door to happiness.

We do not need this and that, we do not need to be this or that, and we do not need to do this or that. Happiness is not complicated—it is simple. Do not cover it, and if it is already covered, uncover it. The magic of life and our happiness lies in ordinary moments lived by your ordinary self.

11

Wonder Knowingly

Law does not evoke much wonder. We encounter a lot of *issues* in law study and practice, but we do not encounter much wonder. We are encouraged to ask questions to elicit information, and we ask questions to get from A to B. When we are hired as lawyers, we are tasked with solving problems. But life is not a problem to be solved; life is a mystery to be lived. And there is a difference between solving a problem and penetrating a mystery. Wonder is an invitation to look beyond the surface. Wonder transforms the ordinary into a mystery. Wonder is the fuel that kindles happiness. The key, then, is to find a sense of wonder in our lives.

Many of us walk through life as if there were very little left to wonder about. This may be in part because we are very busy with the daily tasks of a lawyer or law student. This may also be because we confuse the knowing of names with the knowing of that which is named. But just because we know what to call something does not mean that we know what it actually is. When I say, "That is an ant," I act as though I know what an ant is. I recognized the ant as an ant; I have heard about ants a thousand times and encountered millions of them in my lifetime. By naming it an ant, we have declared reality. Not so. "An ant" is merely the expression of our agreement that we, in the English-speaking part of the world, use the symbol A plus N plus T for any being with these distinguishable features. Nothing more. Naming is necessary to navigate life, but it is a far cry from seeing what truly is. Our symbols are representations of reality, a convenience, not reality itself. Naming should never replace wonder; we should not arrest wonder just because we recall the agreed-upon symbol that makes life manageable. Most of us live as if one excludes the other, so it should not be surprising that we see so little mystery in life.

There is beauty in reason and logic, but a life in which everything is explained and reasoned away is dull. We would exist, but we would not live. I know this from experience: I love the magic in magic tricks, yet I always want to see how a trick works. Every single time I look behind the scenes of a magic trick, I am disappointed. With my knowledge, the magic vanishes; all that remains is a trick. With my knowledge, I become blinded to the magic. A vital part of my "sight" has been taken away from me—the ability to see magic, to wonder.

In our everyday lives, we may think that there is not much left to wonder about, but we are surrounded by opportunities to wonder. We are merely blinded to the magic by our understanding of some of the mechanics and by the perceived mundane nature of some of what we do on a daily basis. The sunrise can still be full of wonder even though we know that it is our rock that is turning to face the sphere of hot plasma, which is heated by nuclear fusion in its core. Just because I know how the iPhone works and what the Internet is, I can still pause to wonder how my mother's beautiful smile and voice radiate over my phone screen into my home from 4,000 miles away.

We often think that it is the job of children to wonder and of adults to pursue knowledge. But how could any scientific discovery be accomplished without wonder? While reason and logic are part of what helps us navigate the world, the ability to wonder is what makes us human. It should not be seen as the activity of the unwise or immature.

Wonder and Wisdom

Does wisdom exclude wonder? Does a perfectly wise being still wonder? Could it be that wonder, in fact, requires wisdom? I do not think that many people would argue with me when I say that Albert Einstein was a pretty wise guy, and we may not often think of him as full of wonder. And yet it was Einstein who said: "The most beautiful thing we can experience is the mysterious. It is the source of all true art and science."

One evening in May 1905, Einstein heard a bell. He had been confounded by a scientific paradox for a decade, and when he gazed up at the tower from which the sound radiated, he wondered: *What would happen if a streetcar raced away from the tower at the speed of light?* Six weeks later, he finished his paper on the special theory of relativity.

It takes wisdom to wonder, to see the mysterious in the mundane. To wonder, we must free ourselves from the arrogance of thinking that we know. It takes wisdom to recognize that we still have questions; that in the greater scheme of things, we know nothing at all. While answers are the expression of knowledge, wonder is the expression of wisdom.

Wonder and Certainty

We strive for certainty and security. Fear despises wonder. We pursue an education in the belief that with our knowledge will come a better job and a secure future. When a global pandemic made many things uncertain, we became anxious and felt insecure. In our quest for security and certainty, we hold on to our knowledge as tight as possible and add to it to increase stability. When my students feel insecure, they seek information that can "cure" this insecurity. In our attempt to add stability to our lives, we suppress wonder. Bertrand Russel said that "[u]ncertainty, in the presence of vivid hopes and fears, is painful, but must be endured if we wish to live without the support of comforting fairytales. It is not good to either forget the questions…, or to persuade ourselves that we have found indubitable answers to them." Our need for certainty must not extinguish our enthusiasm for wonder.

Wonder and Courage

Wonder takes courage. To wonder about my heartbeat before I sleep in my dark bedroom takes some courage. It is strange to fall asleep, wondering why it does not just stop beating. Carl Sagan, the American astronomer, is credited with saying that we "make our world significant by the courage of our questions." Wonder is the courage to fearlessly venture into the unknown. We too often exchange wonder for certainty and security, hoping that it will give us the freedom to enjoy life. It takes courage to look behind the scenes.

To Wonder Is to Sit with a Question

A *koan* is a story, dialogue, question, or statement which is used in Zen practice. "What is the sound of one hand clapping?" is an often-used example. A *koan* requires the Zen practitioner to sit with the question or statement for hours, days, weeks, months, and sometimes even years. I found the notion of sitting with a single question for weeks or months difficult. When I received my first *koan*, my ego took the lead. Off I went down the rabbit hole with my audacious attempt to answer the question. The idea of just sitting with a question escaped me.

Part of the problem was that I could not understand what it meant to "sit with a question." As lawyers, we view questions as things to be answered. Questions on the LSAT, law school exams, and bar exams all are there to be answered. This is what we are taught. The time spent between a question and the answer must be short, especially in an exam. But also in our private lives, as our technological speed has increased, our patience for waiting for answers has decreased. When I was young and had a question that my mom could not answer, we had to find a book in the library. Now, I pick up my phone, and Google gives me the answer instantaneously. The moon is 238,900 miles away—this took 3 seconds. Our patience for unanswered questions is, therefore, waning. We think that sitting with a question reflects inefficiency rather than a virtue to be pursued.

So what does it mean to sit with a question? It asks us to not look for an answer in books or by asking experts but to find "the answer" within our hearts. If there is an answer to be found, it is to be found within us. To sit with a question is to live with it rather than to search for an answer as we usually understand it. It requires us to be patient with having something unresolved and to appreciate that this uncertainty is the very essence of life. But this does not imply passivity. Passively waiting for an answer to come is not questioning. Asking a question is an activity and, as such, requires energy. It requires zeal and awe. It is the magical balance between energetically engaging life and patiently living with the unanswered. A question animates, whereas an answer ends. A question invites and inspires us to engage with life. We question when we wonder, and we wonder when we question.

Wonder and Happiness

What does wonder have to do with happiness? Einstein said that "the most beautiful thing we can experience is the mysterious.... He to whom the emotion is a stranger, who can no longer pause to wonder and stand wrapped in awe, is as good as dead; his eyes are closed." To wonder is to take life in, in its fullest, through every breath. Wonder is not a reaction of the brain but a response of the heart. To wonder is to live.

My depression increases the more life seems mechanical. When I function like a well-tuned machine, I feel hollow, and life seems pointless. I know that I will have to do something about it. I have to pick up a book, not to learn but to wonder. I have to get up in the early mornings and stand outside not simply to watch but to question the sunrise. The everyday madness of our modern life swallows me whole more often than I would like to admit. I need to find space for wonder. If I let up, I will get sucked up by shallowness. And I know that I am not alone; the study or practice of law can entirely consume us unless we carve out space and time for wonder.

I make time to wonder, and I regard my capacity to wonder as a great gift. Happiness does not lie in knowledge; happiness is sandwiched between the known and the unknown. Wonder is the expression of happiness, and happiness the expression of wonder.

Child's Mind

I am grown up in that I take care of my duties. I am responsible, and I earn a living. But beyond that, I like to retain my child's mind. When I was young, I wanted to be older. Now that I am older, I wish to see the world through a child's mind again. Children see the world differently, partly because their brains are not yet fully developed, but also because they think less of the past and the future. Children are more present in the moment than most adults. Children are also much less bothered by expectations and preconceived ideas. Somewhere along the way, the necessary maturity process turns a child into a captive of concepts and categories—an adult.

Children are rough and unpolished and, therefore, much closer to nature than are adults, having been cut, ground, and polished through endless cultivation. While maturation is necessary, the dismantling of our child's mind is not. We develop social skills, technical skills, and soft skills and constantly seek new and improved skills, a process of cultivation that often comes at the expense of spontaneity.

An adult looks at a child and sees an undeveloped mind, a human still to be matured. But through the eyes of a child, it is the adult that looks rather unwise. We think we know better because we have been on this planet longer and have learned and experienced more. But all we know are our preconceived notions and ideas. On the other hand, children know nature, which is why children bounce and sing and dance, play in and with mud, dig, and climb. Why are they so excited about life? We live in the same world, yet while they are running around screaming and laughing with abandon, we sit on the park bench staring at our emails. Who are the fools? The children or us?

"Well, children do not yet have responsibilities," is the usual response. "They do not have bills to pay, mouths to feed, or futures to plan. They are free." True! But they are also much less independent than adults. The child has to be in bed when the parents say, eat what the parents cook, wear what the parents buy, and do what the parents say. With our responsibilities come an enormous amount of freedom. Yet, we use this freedom to build our own cage. Where is the fire? Why do we treat so many things as if they mattered so much? There is no reason not to live playfully. Many of the things that we do on any given day carry with them very little to no weight. Why do we feel the urge to take ourselves and everything that we do so seriously? I walk to the subway station with the seriousness of a heart surgeon. There is nothing playful about that walk. I have to go to work, I cannot miss that train, I must walk fast, I must already plan my dinner and think about paying the month's rent—walk fast, walk fast.

Children see what is in front of them and not what they expect or are expected to see. And children see with their whole being. In a child's facial expression, you can see that which the child is seeing. How wondrous the world must look through a child's mind!

The more we are educated, the less and less we know nature. I know how the rain outside my window developed. I understand the concept of water vapor, clouds, and droplets. But that child that just jumped with both feet and full force into the puddle, much to her mom's dismay, may understand the rain far better than I do.

Knowledge vs. Knowing

Knowledge is important. I would not want to hire an attorney who does not have knowledge in the field in which I need her. Because knowledge is so important in our profession, we study to gain knowledge. But the acquisition of knowledge can compromise the extent to which we know things. Something rather peculiar happened along my journey of acquiring knowledge. The more knowledge I gained, the more insecure I felt.

Life is uncertain. This we have learned from quantum mechanics, a branch of physics that deals with the very small. Werner Heisenberg, a German theoretical physicist, articulated the uncertainty principle in 1927. This principle states that there is a fundamental limit to what we can know about a quantum system. For example, the more precisely we know a particle's position, the less we can know about its momentum, and vice versa. If life is fundamentally uncertain, no matter how much we know, there is always something that we do not know. And the more with think we know, the more we are prone to surprise. The accumulation of knowledge does not lead to happiness. *Knowing* does.

Knowledge is the accumulation of facts, skills, and information through experience and education. Knowledge is important to function well in life. I love to learn and study new things—this is one of my favorite activities. But knowledge is finite and fixed in time. Knowledge comes from a source, either experience or education, and it is accumulated over time. Knowing, on the other hand, is fluid. The *ing* indicates the present. Knowing, therefore, is following the movement, the flow, of the present. It is active rather than static.

Through education, we gain knowledge by learning facts, things that others have found out for us. But knowing is the direct experience of truth that is only possible in full awareness. When we say that someone did something knowingly, we mean that he did what he did in complete awareness. To understand life as an accumulation of facts is not knowing life at all. We can only know life by *knowing* it.

Knowledge can stand in the way of knowing. If I observe a scene, my mind spits out all the knowledge it can find that it deems helpful for the situation. If I get caught up in this spitting out of knowledge, I am incapable of following the flow. The process that we are taught in our education is merely a cultivation of memory that becomes mechanical. But authentic learning is not cumulative; it is a movement of knowing which has no beginning and no end.

Knowledge vs. Wisdom

Knowledge is essential for us to function, but wisdom is essential for us to live happily. Knowledge is power, so we spend our life accumulating knowledge, gained relatively easily by reading and studying. But life is more than the sum of facts. Our education makes us concerned with gaining knowledge. We need knowledge to pass our exams and earn our degrees. Wisdom is secondary. But in life, knowledge is secondary. Knowledge is a tool to function in life. Wisdom, on the other hand, helps us live a healthy and peaceful life. Knowledge is an additive process, but wisdom requires the shedding, the cutting away of that which stands in its way. The more we add, the less we are knowing.

Knowledge vs. Understanding

Do we always understand that to which we know the answer? No! I know that time moves slower for someone in a spaceship approaching the speed of light. But do I Understand it (with a capital U)?

Knowing an answer is altogether different than Understanding. Even understanding an answer intellectually still does not mean Understanding. One has to also Understand the question. But this still is not enough. There is more than a question and an answer. There is a story behind the question, a cause for the question, a path to the question, a path to the answer, a cause for the answer, a story behind the answer. Yet this is still not all. Understanding also includes that which cannot be or is not said—the silence between the question and the answer.

Understanding with the mind and Understanding with your whole being thus are very different things. When a musician understands his instrument, he knows how to achieve a particular sound to produce a specific effect. But that is not what captivates us. The musician Understands something beyond the mechanics. This Understanding is what makes music magical, and it is this kind of Understanding that makes life beautiful. It is more than the sum of all the knowledge. It is beyond knowledge.

While gaining knowledge is important to develop our trade, we need Wisdom, Understanding, and Knowing to appreciate life. Our ability to wonder, our child's mind, is a great treasure that is to be nourished, never neglected.

12

La-La Land

I have spent most of my life in La-La Land. My thought world is boundless and exciting, but it is also a tyrant that controls me with a heavy hand. My depression is closely linked with how trapped I am in my thoughts. There are many days during which I feel that I am not here. Of course I am here, and yet I am not. My wife notices these days quickly. "Where are you today?" she asks. On days on which I feel trapped in my head, I also feel helpless. I do not know of any way out of it. I try to distract myself, but I am really just going through the motions. Sometimes I go back to bed hoping that my mind will have reset when I awake. At other times, I just surrender to the feeling and spend the day on the couch, if possible. These are gruesome days.

The smallest and most benign occurrences can spiral out of control and throw my mind into a loop. It just so happened this weekend. The U.S. Postal Service offers a daily preview email of incoming mail. On Friday, I saw that I was about to receive a letter from my landlord. I was just about to leave the city and knew that I could not receive this letter until after the weekend. For the entire weekend, I was occupied with the contents of the letter. What could it be? Is the landlord selling the building? Am I being evicted? Will I have to move? I told myself to stop worrying about it because there was nothing that I could do at that point, but it just made matters worse. How do you stop your thoughts? My plan B was to look at apartments for sale to see if I could find another place to live if necessary. I thought that if I knew that I could, I would go about my weekend without having to keep worrying. Well, it turned out that this approach made matters even worse because now I not only worried about losing my lease but also about not being able to afford a suitable replacement. My thoughts spiraled out of control due to the pending arrival of a letter that turned out to be the announcement that the laundry room would be closed for a week. I am an excellent mental movie maker: the closing of the laundry room turned into the loss of my home and a move into a cockroach-infested dungeon.

As lawyers we must think. We look to thoughts; we toss them around; we revere great thoughts. But there is a danger of putting too much emphasis on our thoughts. Most of them have nothing in it for us. Thoughts are tools we use in our profession but they must be managed well as to not let them dismantle our lives. As Audre Lorde said: "The master's tools will never dismantle the master's house."

Over the past few months, I learned more about my thoughts than I have learned in the last thirty-nine years. I have done this merely by observing them. My starting point was to accept that just like it is the heart's job to pump, it is the brain's job to think. To say to someone, "Just stop thinking about it!" is as fruitless as pushing the elevator button multiple times. The brain cannot stop thinking unless it is dead. Frustration arises from the impossible pursuit of ceasing the brain's natural function, which actually makes matters worse. To stop a particular thought, you must think even more about the very thought that you want to stop. It is like holding a fish in your hand—the more you try to hold it, the more the fish wiggles and jumps in your hand. Instead of trying to arrest thoughts, we must let them do what they naturally do. All we have to do is to put the fish back into the water.

Clouds

Some fifteen years ago, I decided to jump out of a plane. Since I still had many plans for my life, I decided to do so with a parachute. I will never forget the feeling of my feet dangling out of the plane while I was sitting at the edge of the door. With a tiny little push of the body, I was airborne. The initial tingle in the tummy subsided once I reached terminal velocity—the point at which air resistance is equal to the force of gravity. From that moment on, I did not accelerate, and it felt like I was flying. I was falling towards earth without a care in the world. My jumping-off point was pretty high, so it was inevitable that I would have to make my way through clouds. Clouds can look intimidating close up, especially if you are not protected by a plane's fuselage. Approaching a cloud in freefall feels like running straight towards a wall, but by this point you do not have a choice.

Curiously, what looked so scary from the outside was barely noticeable while inside. I saw clouds approach below me and then disappear above me, but I never really noticed flying through them. What looked solid from a distance felt like nothing while in it. I could not feel, touch, or see them. It was only later, when I watched the video, that I was able to confirm that I indeed did fall through clouds.

Our thoughts are just like those clouds. They are not solid, stable things, but brief energy coming and going. It is not necessary to hold on to them; in fact we can't, we can only fly through them. The thought will disappear just as the clouds do. Thoughts have no meaning other than the meaning that we give them. When we recognize their fleeting nature, they become less important.

Beyond Clouds

Dogen Zenji, an influential Zen master, once wrote that we should "[t]hink of non-thinking." I tried to follow his advice during my meditation. "Just think of non-thinking." But how does one do this? If I think of non-thinking, is that not a thought? How do I know if I do not think? If I say to myself, "I am not thinking," I am expressing a thought. This is beyond me, I thought. "Beyond!" "Why not go beyond thought?"

To notice the fleeting nature of our thoughts helps us detach from them rather than indulge in them. In a one-hour meditation block, my mind typically goes through myriad thoughts. When thoughts arise, I feel inclined to indulge each of them, but I have learned to just let them be, to return to my breath, and to let thoughts pass. It turns out that if you let thoughts pass and stop giving them meaning, they disappear just as fast as they arose. Thoughts are ephemeral. Beyond my thoughts, the mind is always clear. If I stop indulging them, like clouds in the sky they will pass without a trace.

Muddy Waters

The other day I was driving over the Queensboro Bridge toward the city. After nine years of living in New York, I still get excited about seeing the city from that bridge. No matter how often I cross it, it always feels like the very first time. This time, however, I was struck by a rather curious thought. "I have never truly seen the city!" How could I possibly think that? I see the city every morning when I wake up. But all of a sudden, I realized that all I have ever seen is my commentary about the city: "The city is gorgeous, it is loud, it is dirty, it is crowded, it is exciting, etc."

All I have ever "seen" in my life is my reflection and judgment about things. I have not "seen" without thinking a thought about that which I see. "Would it be possible," I thought, "to truly see something as it is, rather than what I think about it?" I do not have an answer yet, but I realized a flaw in my view of life. This thought experiment showed me that fundamentally we never truly attend to what *is* but only to what we think about it. Whether good or bad, green or blue, our thoughts are merely commentary. Even though

things exist out there in the world, we experience only our sub-
jective interpretation. We look at our very own superimposition
and mistake this for what is. We do not "see" life, we comment on
life, and in doing so we separate ourselves from it. Seeing a beach,
as in "I am looking at this beautiful beach," is very different from
sitting on a beach. We must feel what we are experiencing as it is
and not simply as it is named. Kilian Jornet, a Spanish professional
sky runner, talked about his move to Norway in a TV interview.
He explained that many mountains in Norway do not have names.
He reflected that in the naming we lose something: "In France, you
climb Mont Blanc; in Norway, you climb a mountain." I know that
I have yet to "see" the world. Even if I walk around thinking I have
seen this before, I know in my heart that there is still a world to be
seen, right here in front of me.

I See You!

Thoreau asked, "[c]ould a greater miracle take place than for us to
look through each other's eyes for an instant?" He did not say *into*
each other's eyes; he said *through* them. We look into each other's
eyes all the time and find only the surface of the other—the mask:
the words, the behavior, the clothes, and what we think of them.
To leap beyond the surface and truly see the other, not in relation
to us but just as they are at this very moment, is the true meaning
of "I see you."

I have seen my wife of eight years much more than anyone in my
life. Yet have I ever truly seen her—just as she is? I have seen only
my reflections about her and my emotions toward her.

We have seen even less of most of the people we engage with
on a day-to-day basis. We make judgments, and we take the information that we have about the person to mean that this is, in fact,
the person that is right in front of us. We hear words and observe
behavior and clothing. Very often, we use outdated information to
make a judgment about who they are right now. "He was the CEO

of ABC and then left to spend more time with his family. His family *is* very important to him." By now, he may be getting a divorce, and if we would only pierce through his eyes, we would see his pain. Instead, we see our own processing of information—current and past—the result of which we interpret as seeing the person as he is right now. But to truly see a person, we must follow the living and breathing organism that is a human. To truly see means to be able to follow the movement.

It is this inability to see that explains in part why humans are so biased. We see a man in a suit and react towards him differently than we do towards the man in dirty, ripped jeans with a plastic bag in his hands. In neither instance do we see the person, only our judgments about him. How much less biased we could be if we would genuinely say: "I see you." This may not be something we can readily do, but that should not stop us from trying. Having an awareness about our limitations in seeing can already go a long way. If we then try our best to see through someone's eyes instead of just at them, who knows what treasures we might find.

Beyond Past and Future

Fantasizing provided an escape mechanism from the boredom of my childhood. And escape I did. I spent nearly every waking hour in my imagination. Through this world of make-believe, I built a refuge, a haven against the storms of my personal life, my own paracosm. And I did this well into my thirties. While others lived, I stayed in my make-believe world.

Because I was never really there, I have very little memory of my past, only bits and pieces of disjointed moments. When you escape your own life, how can you say you have lived? When I was about thirty-two years old, I turned all my dreams into reality—the two merged. I had everything that I had ever wanted and no more reason to escape. But by turning dreams into life, I robbed myself of the only thing I knew—my imagination, and even my incentive to imagine. Now that I no longer wanted to escape, I did not know how to deal with the present. I felt as helpless as a newborn. For my whole life, I attended to what might be; at thirty-two, I wanted to attend to what is. By thinking about my future, I separated myself from what was. Now, I needed to learn to merge with what is.

Law students, and probably many attorneys, spend a lot of time in the future, mostly worrying about it. The separation between imagination and reality, between the future and here, is thought. Fundamentally, the very fabric of reality is one endless *here*. It is only thought that carries us to the past and future. Reality knows no such thing. To sit in the here and now and not wander off into fantasy land is the most challenging task I have ever attempted. But I know that I have to do this because I do not want to lie on my death bed not having lived a single moment. During those very few instances in which I was "just sitting" on my cushion without being trapped in thought, the "here" was completely sufficient and beautiful beyond description.

The Power to Change Mount Everest

I spent a mini vacation in Long Beach, New York. I love the off-season, when it is deserted yet still warm enough to spend time on the beach. On one particular day, the beach seemed exceptionally beautiful. It was cold enough for a hoodie but warm enough to walk barefoot and graze the water. I saw living crabs instead of their usual dead body parts. I sat on the jetties and enjoyed the dancing of the waves.

The very next day I went back to the beach, only this time it was not there. It was still cold enough for a hoodie and warm enough to walk barefoot and graze the water. There were waves, but this time no dancing. I saw no live crabs, only their dead body parts. I could not smell the sea. The sound of the waves was muffled. Both light and sound conspired to stop short of reaching me. Where was my beach from yesterday? This beach did nothing for me.

The beach, of course, had not changed; I had. The beach was just as it was the day before, in all its glory, but I was trapped in my thoughts and unable to see it. I was depressed that day, and I tried to pull myself out of my mind and into the moment, but I could not do so. These moments are scary. Fortunately, they are also the source of much wisdom. Our experience of the world is not determined by the circumstances in which we find ourselves, but by the mind. The beach is the beach is the beach. But I experienced it differently from one day to the next, not because of the beach, but because of my very own mind. If it works from good to bad, it must work the other way, as well.

When we walk into the law school building or office, what we encounter depends on our thoughts. The law school building, office, boardroom, or courtroom can be as beautiful as a beach or as ugly as we want it to be.

Whenever life seems stressful, scary, and dangerous, we must stop and ask ourselves earnestly: "Is it life that is like that, or am I confusing my mental movie with it?" Our mind is not always an accurate representation of life. As lawyers we become so attached to the world of thought that we can easily miss the world that is.

13

Inside a Bag of Skin

Before I started meditating, the idea of sitting in front of a wall, motionless, seemed utterly ludicrous. What is the point? Is it not a complete waste of our valuable time here on this earth? Yet so many people today and through the ages have testified to its value and importance. They cannot all be wrong, so I decided to give it a try. Until that point in my life, I had been trying to find answers in books, education, wealth, power, mentors, family, and friends to the questions that had haunted me my entire life—"What do I want to do with my life?" "Why am I here?" "What am I supposed to do?" "What is the meaning of life?" Nowhere could I find anything close to answers. The only place that was left to look was inside. "When you can't find the answer out there," I thought, "you can give up or turn inwards." So I sat down in front of a wall, stopped moving, and looked.

Time dilation predicts that time is slower for a moving object than a non-moving object. The effect of time dilation is confirmed by several experiments, such as the Hafele-Keating experiments of 1971. Atomic clocks were flown on airplanes traveling in opposite directions. The time differences shown on the clocks precisely matched the predictions from relativity.

The concept of time dilation reminds me of what happens when we run around as if our pants are on fire. Our fast-paced environment and the ability and perceived necessity of moving around faster and faster come at a cost. Just like motion in space alters the flow of time, running around alters our perception of life. The more we speed up, the less depth we can penetrate, and the more shallow life starts to feel. When energy is directed towards movement, we do not have the energy to perceive depth. When we look outside a moving train, the environment that we observe lacks depth. It is a continuous flow of images devoid of that detail which makes it special.

A happy life is found in depth, not on the surface. To perceive life's depth, mystery, and beauty, we must stand still and use all our energy to look straight at it. This standing still must involve not only a motionless body but also a still mind. We must look at life with every fiber of our being.

The First Law of Thermodynamics states that energy is always conserved. While it cannot be created or destroyed, it can certainly be diverted. We live life, however, as if we had an endless supply of energy. We find training, practices, supplements, tips, and tricks to have more energy. But nothing we do will give us *more* energy. The notion that our supply of energy can be increased is the same fallacy as that our time on this planet is infinite. Neither is true. There is only so much time and so much energy, and both must be managed well. It is up to us how we use our allotment. If we choose to use our energy running around chasing shadows, we must be content with only perceiving life's surface. If we choose instead to use some of our energy to pierce the surface, we may find that meaning and happiness have been there all along, and only our busyness prevented us from seeing it. We cannot both run around and perceive depth. We must stop to see.

This by no means suggests a stationary, complacent, or relaxed state. To pierce through life's surface is anything else but a relaxing pursuit. It requires a great deal of energy, determination, and focus. When we see a Zen monk sitting on his cushion, he may look relaxed, but the sweat dripping from his forehead reveals his true efforts.

Entangled

Individualism is what appealed to me when I moved to the U.S. To rely only on myself and to not be dependent on anyone or anything empowered me to become whoever I chose to be. I come from a country with a robust social support system. Even though I benefitted from it, I felt that my personal and professional development was inhibited. I felt that if I had to keep living within that system, I could not be free. Is the focus on the rugged individualist the answer? Law students and attorneys often feel lonely and isolated. They are working alone, in a setting of constant competition. But when we penetrate into life's depths, we discover that we are not the independent, rugged individualists we pride ourselves on being. We see clearly that we are interconnected and interdependent, even amidst competition. To experience the connectedness that is the basis of life will make us feel less lonely, less lost. Working collegially with classmates and counterparts helps and is a much-valued trait in the profession.

While I tried to understand this universe we live in and perused physics books, I stumbled upon something that was quite baffling. Experts in quantum mechanics, the physics of the stuff things are made of, have been trying for years to identify life's building blocks. We discovered the atom, the electron, and the entire periodic table. We then felt content until we started to observe the behavior of the very small, and the world did not make much sense anymore. It turns out that the world of the small behaves quite strangely and very differently from what we observe on a day-to-day basis. But the big things we observe daily are made of the small stuff. That is a bit of a conundrum, to say the least.

In quantum physics, entangled particles remain connected so that actions performed on one affect the other, even when separated by great distances. This principle, demonstrated by both Einstein and Schrödinger in 1935, occurs when pairs or groups of particles are generated in such a way that the state of each particle is correlated with the others. Within an entangled system, the simple act of measuring a single particle will influence its entangled partners. The observer, therefore, must measure the state of the quantum system as a whole. The phenomenon so baffled even Albert Einstein that he called it "spooky action at a distance." How what we learned about the world of the small translates into the world of the big is still problematic. But quantum entanglement offers a metaphor. We should not view ourselves as isolated creatures on a lonely little planet in a cold, vast universe but as interdependent parts of a great whole. We should embrace this concept in our lives whenever the opportunity arises.

If a virus like COVID-19 can tell us one thing, it is that we are part of a giant web. Our actions are so intertwined that the virus ran through the world with breakneck speed. Amala Wrightson Sensei said: "When someone in Wuhan gets sick, someone in New Zealand loses his job."

In addition to being connected, we need each other to survive. The truck driver, the gas station attendant, the grocery store clerk, the staff in public transportation, the gas delivery person, the car mechanic, the firefighter, the garbageman, the postal worker, and the health care worker all are essential to our lives. Without each and every one of them, we would be lost. We do not think much about it during our regular life. The trash gets picked up, and we likely have never thought of that person before. Now we wonder, who is this person who still goes to work every day while the rest of us barricade inside? We wonder, what would it look like if she does not show up anymore?

I love my personal liberty but I do not want to feel isolated. I enjoy feeling connected to something larger than me. The interplay between personal liberty and interdependence is shown clearly during a pandemic. A sense of interdependence can help control the virus, whereas a myopic focus on personal liberty will spread the virus. When we wear a mask, we acknowledge the interdependence and connectedness that govern our lives. By the very act of physically distancing ourselves from others, we acknowledge our interdependence and how our behavior affects other human beings. We express connectedness by an outward expression of separation. I cover myself to protect you.

While my wife and I were getting ready to shelter in place during the pandemic, I reached the peak of my stress level. The thought of staying at home and away from other humans under "social distancing" guidelines depressed me. I was operating under the principle of protecting myself from the virus. Stay away so that you do not get sick! Then I talked to my eighty-three-year-old grandmother on the phone in Germany. She was isolated, as well. She was not receiving visitors or shopping, activities that she loves so much. After I hung up, I realized that I am not sheltered in place to protect myself. I am thirty-nine, healthy, and active. I am staying in to protect others, like my grandmother, who are more vulnerable. From that moment on, everything became more comfortable. Going into shelter was not a lonesome act, but an act of compassion for the wellbeing of my fellow humans and respect for the web in which we live. The sadness dissipated, and I felt less isolated. To the contrary, I felt connected to the community more than ever. By staying away, I was reaching out. This greater purpose calmed my anxiety and stress and brought me back to a place of contentment.

Even though we compete against other law students or other junior associates, we can still acknowledge and cherish our interconnectedness. We are all in the same boat called life.

Not Just Necessity

We are connected with each other in part because we need each other. We need each other on a personal and emotional level—the touch of someone you love, the smell and warmth of a body close to you.

I have had the great fortune to travel the world for work. I have seen many beautiful places, met many interesting and amazing people, and learned a great deal from other cultures. This has been an incredibly enriching and rewarding endeavor. One day while in Mexico City, I called my mother, who was 5,919 miles away in Germany. I was sitting in an Uber on my way to the hotel. My mom was at my brother's house, and I could hear him and his family in the background. While I was looking outside the window, I shared with my mom what I was seeing. I tried to describe Mexico City from a car to someone who has never been there. I sent pictures to my brother and the kids to show them where I was. This sharing with my family is what made what I experienced "alone" in the car beautiful. I tried to imagine seeing the world without having people I love to share it with. How would that feel? How would it feel to see a beautiful sunset in Ipanema, Rio de Janeiro, without having someone to share it with? Shared experiences are so much more valuable than moments experienced alone. Even sharing it after the fact, the retelling and reliving, are part of the experience. Connecting the experience to the whole is what makes it magical. A sunset seen while feeling connected and loved is a beautiful sunset. A sunset seen while feeling lonely, disconnected, and unloved is sad. The same event can be experienced in many different ways.

The legal profession offers many opportunities to connect our work to the web in which we live. We can work both for ourselves and for the whole. We can turn a stressful job into a satisfying mission simply by appreciating our interconnectedness.

I Am Not Me Without You

We exist in relation to our environment. It is difficult to say what is the unchangeable core of me, if such a thing even exists. Am I the same when I am living in the woods as when I am living in New York City? Whether we are entangled particles or not, we are connected in more ways than meet the eye. All phenomena lack their own inherent existence because their very existence is dependent on the conditions that give rise to them. We are connected to everything around us, and we are who we are because of where we are, what we are doing, and with whom we are doing it. To look at ourselves without looking around us is to not look at ourselves at all. If we cannot see the whole, we do not see clearly. Whenever we feel lonely, we have to remind ourselves that we are part of a gigantic cosmic web that nourishes us.

14

Dust in the Wind

I both despise and crave change. When my days feel like *Groundhog Day*, I get bored and restless. Life becomes stale, like a song that has been played too many times. I have to do something to change things up. But change terrifies me.

We function in life because of its apparent stability. When I flip the light switch in the morning, the room is bright. When I go to the subway, the train will come around the same time. When I go to work, the building and my colleagues are still there. We build our habits and rhythms around the stability of our everyday lives. It makes us feel safe. When something in our "stable" environment changes, we are uprooted. Starting law school and entering the profession are examples of enormous changes in our lives.

When my family plans to visit me in the U.S., I spend weeks leading up to it feeling exhilarated. I plan our days ahead of time, and I simulate the visit in my mind hundreds of times. Just before they arrive, the excitement is almost unbearable. I arrive at the airport hours before they arrive, just to be on the safe side. I look at every single person coming out of customs even though my family's plane has not even arrived yet. And then, when the door finally opens and I recognize the familiar faces that give me so much comfort, something terrible happens. From this moment on, I am terrified. I know that my family will have to leave me again and that I will stand in this very building, this time on the departure level, with tears in my eyes, having to say goodbye. I know that this visit is impermanent. It will end, and I do not want it to end. It is not that I want my family to live with me; what I want is this visit, this very moment, this happiness, this excitement, to not change. I cling to this very moment with all my might.

Moving from Germany to the U.S. was the most significant change in my life. It was both exciting and frightening. However, it was a change that I initiated and that I anticipated and prepared for. This is not the kind of change that causes distress. Being confronted with unwanted or unexpected change is what generates feelings of unrest. The COVID-19 pandemic forced changes upon every one of us. Law classes moved online; law school buildings, offices, and courts closed; gyms closed; restaurants closed; and travel was restricted. It was an opportunity, albeit an unwelcomed one, to contemplate impermanence. Just a week before the lockdown, I competed in the American Open in Columbus, Ohio, a weightlifting competition for which I trained for two years. It was supposed to be my path to the national and ultimately to the world competitions. A week after this competition, I could not train anymore because my gym was literally covered with plywood. Training had been the most important activity in my life for years. In the blink of an eye, it was gone. At first, I thought of it as a short break; it was inconceivable that seven months down the road, I would still not have access to my training hall. When, if, and how my training will return is uncertain, as is my competitive season. I find myself without that anchor in my life. Obviously, this is a minor inconvenience compared to the losses others have had to face during this pandemic. But it is this very fact that makes it such a good example for this chapter. I did not lose anything of great significance, like my health, a family member, or a job. Yet this minor loss in my daily routine threw me completely out of balance. I was not prepared for and never even conceived of the possibility of this change.

"It really goes to show you."

I just got off the phone with a friend, and she dropped the line I have used many times myself but now abhor. She told me about an acquaintance who fell off the stairs after drinking too much. The next day she collapsed in the bathroom and died of a brain aneurism. "It really goes to show you," my friend said, "you must be grateful and live every day to the fullest."

We use stories like this to wake us up, albeit temporarily. This sudden brush with impermanence makes us pause. We realize then and there that we are wasteful with the life that we have been granted. But since looking into impermanence is painful, we quickly move on without giving this topic the attention it deserves.

We take the wrong lesson from stories like these. Rather than saying, "It really goes to show you, you must be grateful and live every day to the fullest," we should be saying, "It really goes to show you, we must come to terms with impermanence."

Impermanence also can help us get through difficult moments in law study or practice. As we grieve the impermanence of things we treasure, we can take solace in the fleeting nature of difficult moments. As the saying goes, this too shall pass.

Impermanence Is Stable

Everything around us changes. Only change itself does not change. Some change is observable, like the guacamole turning brown. Some change less so, like a stone. But one only has to walk on the beach to be reminded that even something as seemingly solid as a rock is, at this very moment, changing. Just because some things change more slowly than others does not mean that they are not changing. Scientists speculate that the sun will die in about five billion years. Despite this, we hold on to our illusion of stability. Is it possible for us not only to accept change but to recognize that impermanence is that very feature that makes life special and beautiful?

Beauty in Change

The time that I spend with my family when they visit is filled with activity, laughter, and good spirits. We all appreciate those special few days for which we waited so long and which soon will be over. In an ironic twist, the impermanence that I so loathe is the very thing that makes these moments unique. The beauty is in its finitude.

As I am writing these words, I am watching leaves fall from the trees. The summer is a memory, and the fall announces its intentions. I cannot help but feel sad that summer is over; gone are the days I sit outside long into the evenings. But I also love the crisp air and the red leaves that autumn brings, and I know that one must yield to the other.

It is easy to understand the inevitability of change on a rational level, but quite another to find beauty therein. But change is beautiful. To see someone dancing is to see her assume a pose and let that pose go. It is a coming and going of poses. To watch someone on stage for two hours holding one pose would be painfully boring. We need to let each pose die to see the dance. And it is this dancing, this coming and going, that makes life gorgeous. Demanding life to hold one pose would make it a terribly boring performance. Being frustrated by impermanence is like being frustrated by the sun setting. We do not take any issue with the sun doing its dance, so why do we take issue with the rest of life dancing?

We cannot make permanent that which is not. By taking hold of a moment, we interrupt its unfolding, the coming and going that, in the end, makes life beautiful.

Stability in Change

Is it at all possible to find stability or comfort in change? We must. Given its constancy, we cannot allow ourselves to be thrown off by change.

Change is life, and without change, there is no life. Life is a process, a coming and going, a receiving and losing, a growing and a dying. Life is not fixed but fluid. To try to avoid change is to try to avoid living. The grasping of something that will—that must—change is futile. To hold on to a moment is to kill the moment. To hold on to someone you love is to destroy that love. We can flourish in the instability of life by moving with change rather than fighting it.

No drug, no religion, and no science will help us change change. Who would encourage a friend to fight a non-winnable battle? We must surrender to change. Ninety-eight percent of the atoms in our body are replaced yearly. We are not just part of an environment that changes; we ourselves are change. We have come to believe that happiness requires and flourishes only in a stable environment. But what we perceive as stable is as impermanent as everything else. Suppose happiness requires stability and flourishes only in a stable environment. In that case, we must welcome and embrace change rather than avoid it because it is the only thing that is stable.

Conditioned Love

"I love you just the way you are" is a beautiful line from a beautiful song, a line we love to hear. We are accepted, respected, and loved for who we are. But what if we change? "I love you just the way you are" implies a fixed state—the way you are right now. How many times have friendships fallen apart and marriages dissolved because "She changed so much. She is not the person I married 20 years ago."

Human beings change because we are part of everything that changes. I am not the same person I was twenty years ago and not quite the person I was before the pandemic. I am not even the same person I was yesterday because yesterday I was in a terrible mood, and today I am in great spirits. When we truly love someone unconditionally, we love him for what he truly is—a living being who is change. We cannot cling to people as they are now.

By asking another human to be unchanging, we ask them to stop being human. To love someone unconditionally means to live with her and the inevitable changes. If we try to hold on to the person we met five years ago in a bar, we will suffer because that person may not exist anymore. "I love you the way you will be at every moment" is unconditional love. And even if change parts two people, one can still respect and love the other. People do not change at the same pace or in the same direction. To be angry at someone for changing is like being mad at the leaves for changing their color.

Today Yes, Tomorrow No!

Nothing frustrates me more than lifting 108 pounds one day easily, while the very next day missing it several times. My weightlifting training is a rollercoaster, and I never quite know how my training will go on a particular day. The same is true for everything else that I do. Today I might say that I would love to spend the weekend at the beach and tomorrow I may prefer a lazy weekend on the sofa. Today I may have a lot of compassion and patience with my students, tomorrow I may easily be irritated. I am not that rock-solid person that I wish I were. My thoughts, feelings, desires, passions, and wishes are all as impermanent as everything else in the universe. I do not want to get into whether there is an unchangeable "I," a personality that remains solid through the years. I would like to think so, but I am not willing to bet my life's savings on it. Regardless, we can all agree that how we are today and how we were yesterday, ten, fifteen, or twenty years ago can be quite different, sometimes dramatically so. This is one of the many facts of life that I have been working the longest to truly accept. I am frustrated with myself because I feel unstable and weak. Sometimes I do not understand why I underperform in a task in which I usually excel, why I am patient one day but not the next, why I sometimes feel like meeting people and other times prefer hiding under a blanket. How can I change my mind within minutes? I dislike this part of myself, and I have fought for years to become that stable being in complete control of herself. I kept failing. I must accept that I am change.

Lawyers tend to be very hard on themselves, often serving as their own worst critics. While this can be a helpful form of self-reflection, it can also lead to defeatism and a sense of pessimism. When we under-perform with respect to a matter or a task, we should do what we can to learn from the experience and move on, knowing that a single project does not define us. Each of us has bad days, and these too are impermanent.

By no means is this to be taken as "I am what I am, and I am not working on myself." On the contrary, to be able to develop and to work on ourselves is a beautiful gift that should be honored. But we should not be frustrated with our ordinary human tendency to change.

So Does the Heart Not Move?

"If you don't feel sad when things change, does it mean that you have withdrawn and do not care anymore?" The question makes sense only if one assumes that feeling sad and accepting change are mutually exclusive: if you accept change, you will never be sad; if you are sad, you have not accepted change. This equation is ludicrous. Because I am human, I will, of course, sometimes feel sad. One can feel sad and let go simultaneously, without any contradiction. The reason we assume otherwise is that we are conditioned to think that we must cling to that which we love. But in love, clinging is not necessary. I can feel sadness and accept change at the same time. Until the very last day, I will have tears in my eyes when I have to say goodbye to my family at the airport. Yet I will keep saying goodbye. With tears in my eyes, I will let the moment slip away. Then I will turn around, take a deep breath, and embrace the next moment. A human whose heart does not move cannot be a happy human. To be a healthy human being, I must not suppress my emotions. But I can work on myself until I can courageously and gracefully let moments, experiences, and humans go. I can learn to gratefully accept that I am part of a beautiful dance.

Do I dare say that the impermanence of life is what makes it beautiful? Or to frame it more aggressively: Is death what makes life livable? When I think about the impermanence of my life and of those I love, I choke. It is too painful. Yet, life's impermanence—death—is part of life and something we cannot avoid addressing.

The Art of Dying

Do I want to die? No. Am I going to die? Yes. To reconcile the two is to unlock freedom. For that, we must look into the eye of death.

I Will Die

One day I will die. I can say these words calmly and peacefully: one day, I will die! But since an early age, I have been terrified of death—my own and that of those I love. Death is eerie—not the act of dying itself, but the endlessness of the nothingness that will come after my own death and the finitude that comes with the death of those I love. How can this nothingness and finitude not throw us into a deep depression?

I have been tiptoeing around this chapter since I started writing this book. I do not want to think about death, and I do not want to write about death. Death is something that happens to others, not to me. Tolstoy writes in *The Death of Ivan Ilyich*: "Caius is a man, men are mortal, therefore Caius is mortal." His character Ivan Ilyich understood this syllogism but felt that it somehow would not apply to him. I felt the same way.

When I tell my friends that I am working on the chapter on death for my book on happiness, they are dumbfounded. "Why are you talking about death when you are trying to help others be happy?" With this question, they stick the needle right into the heart of the issue. How can there ever be true happiness without coming to terms with life's finitude? It is this coming to terms that may help us appreciate life to the greatest extent, even when burdened with studies or work.

If or When?

It is a certainty that we all are going to die. The only uncertainty is when. This may be my last day or my last hour on this earth. I know it on a rational level, but my heart does not allow itself to go there. How can someone possibly make peace with this cruel fact? Right after my last five-day silent meditation retreat, my wife told me that our next-door neighbor, a young, funny woman full of life, went to bed and never woke up. My wife saw her being taken out of the building on a stretcher. "How can this be?" I said, "I just saw her in the gym." While writing this, I imagine her children emptying out her apartment, an entire life packed up in boxes. They have tears in their eyes, but even those tears will one day disappear, and their lives will resume some level of normalcy. I had just spent a week in silence to find some peace in my battered soul, and with one line, I was knocked off my feet again. The cruelty and randomness of death brought back all of the torment I had managed to silence for a week.

I was distressed that life just kept on going on as if nothing happened. Death feels so horrendous and its finitude so painful that I expect the earth to shake or the sky to darken with every single death. But no such thing happens. The day our neighbor died went on like any other day. You could be in your apartment just fifteen feet away from death and notice nothing. The sun still shines, people are on their bikes, others enjoy ice cream. This death meant a lot to those close to her but nothing to the universe at large. It was just another thing that the universe does: it gives birth, it lets die. Life went on as if nothing happened. How dare life do that? A human being died without warning or reason. How can the universe not care?

Either life is cruel, I thought, or it is because death is not the dark monster that we make it out to be. It is not that this person did not matter; this person mattered as much and as little as every one of us. It is that death itself is insignificant. Death is all around us, and the reason why the earth keeps spinning and the sun keeps shining is that death is not a monster we must destroy but a natural occurrence we must appreciate. The only way to avoid death is to not be born.

While family and friends were mourning her loss, the neighbors and I suffered because of fear. "This can happen to me at any time." No one likes to admit this reaction, and we may not even be aware of it. What stirs up our emotions is the closeness of death and the reminder that "this could have been my mom or me." We do a great job of suppressing the inevitability of death, but when it comes so close, our wall gets a crack. Whether we are aware of it or not, we are affected by mortality awareness. In a psychosocial experiment in Arizona, judges were tasked with recommending a fine for defendants accused of a misdemeanor. In the instructions, half of the judges were provided with questions that required reflection on their own mortality. When the judges were reminded of the prospect of their own demise, they enforced the law more vigorously. On average, the fines issued by those judges were nine times that of the control group. Mortality awareness guides the way we live even though we go on pretending that death is not happening. How can we talk about happiness when we cannot live with the basic facts of life?

When I heard the news of our neighbor's death, my peace was gone, and I sat slouched in a chair. Then I started a thought experiment. How would we feel about death if each and every one of us had exactly the same amount of time on this earth? Would that make us feel better about death? I believe so.

"Just like an unending song gets tedious fast, so would an unending life lose its beauty," I thought. "How would life without death even feel? Who really wants to live forever?" It is not so much death itself that troubles us; it is the uncertainty and randomness that troubles us. On any given day, one can go to bed and not wake up. Uncertainty is what makes death so cruel. No one wants infinite time on this earth. What we want is to have as much time as we want. We want to have a say in this. We want to be the master of our life and of our death. We seek control.

So we go about our lives pretending that we have as much time as we want, as if we have control. This is a delusion that inhibits happiness because it interferes with living an honest life. The loss of this delusion may enable us to put our daily annoyances into better perspective.

Making Peace With Death

There is nothing wrong with finitude. Finitude is life. Everything ends at some point, and meaning is found in the moments between the coming and the going. Marcus Aurelius pointed out that finitude and impermanence are not tragic, but the context in which true value can be created. The beauty and meaning of a song or a movie lie between the beginning and the end. We barely notice finitude because it is such an inherent feature of life. My writing of this book will come to an end, the pandemic will come to an end, this autumn will come to an end, my tummy ache will come to an end, the cake I am eating will come to an end, my law study came to an end, the bar exam came to an end, and so on. Finitude is not only part and parcel of life, but the awareness of our finitude—our death—is what makes life rich. Suppressing it makes life one of delusion. To suppress our own mortality is to suppress living. How can one be happy living a delusional life?

Bruce Lee said that to learn to die is to be liberated from it. Donald Robertson noted that to learn how to die is to unlearn how to be a slave. If we try to make permanent that which is finite, we are fighting a lost battle. A life engaged in such a war is no life; it is the refusal of life. Happiness can never be found in denial. We must make peace with death.

Death to Self

There is death we seek to avoid, and then there is death we should be striving for. I am a self-preservation expert. I am careful not to kill myself in any undertaking. This seems a pretty healthy approach conducive to long living. But more than the preservation of my physical body—I jumped out of a plane, ride a unicycle through Manhattan, and hold many pounds of iron straight over my neck—I am an expert in preserving my Self with a capital S—my ego, my identity, the "I" that distinguishes me from others. Whatever I do, I am sure not to injure that Self.

Even my most successful artistic and athletic endeavors have been mediocre at best. One reason for this undoubtedly is my unwillingness to work more than absolutely necessary. But beyond that, it was my self-consciousness, a form of self-preservation that can make life superficial. Being self-conscious means that we are acutely aware of ourselves as ourselves. We are conscious of our Self moving in time. A great actor is someone who is completely absorbed in the part that she is playing. In other words, a great actor is an actor who completely drops her Self. A mediocre actor is one who owns her role but does not let go of her Self completely. The performance feels contrived, stale. I was quite successful as a television and movie actress, considering my mediocre acting. I played my parts decently. But it always remained Me playing a role. It was never a true artistic endeavor. The same goes for singing. A song is beautiful when there is only a song, rather than the dualism of a person singing a song. A poet, too, must completely be the poem. If there is an "I" writing a poem, one can feel this duality. The poem does not knock you off your feet. But if the poem comes from a place of no-Self, its beauty is ungraspable.

So we are both self-aware and attached to this awareness. We yearn to feel individual, a real person that is seen and respected by others. We are attached to the feeling of "I," to the feeling that "I" exist, that "I" am living "my" life. This self-consciousness is normal and, in most cases, does not hinder a normal life. But it can stand

111

in the way of happiness. Our clinging to the Self prevents us from engaging in genuine expression. We must allow ourselves to let the Self rest, or even die all together so that we can be a moment.

Lawyers may have special difficulty with this concept. We tend to have large egos, fueled by the competitive nature of law school and the profession, and the need to be assertive in many contexts. Letting go of this ego may be a challenge but is essential to happiness.

Being a Moment

Not everyone wants to pursue artistic or athletic endeavors, but we all want to feel alive. Feeling alive means that we feel animated. It is an active state. Clinging to the Self, to the "I," on the other hand, is a rigid, non-moving state—a holding on to a point in time. Feeling alive requires letting go of this artificial point in time. We must let the "Self" die so that we can live. What we call Self is a living and moving process, a process that is change itself. If we cling to an imagined Self, by the time we feel we possess it, it is already gone. So we are clinging to something from the past. To be alive, we cannot hold on but must allow ourselves to move with each moment as it comes.

Every day, every hour, and every second, I am self-conscious as in conscious of my Self. When I eat a pizza, it is me eating a pizza. If I sit and meditate, it is me doing an act called sitting. If I sit on the beach watching the ocean, it is me on sand watching an ocean. I am always aware of myself being in a setting and doing an activity. If I let my Self go, if I let my Self die, then there is no "me" sitting on sand watching an ocean; there is only a moment—the ocean, the salt, the sun, the sand, the air, the birds, the people, together creating that one moment. There is not this and that; there is only all. If we hold on to a Self that is acting in an environment surrounded by other Selves, we cut one moment into bits and pieces. When we separate this moment into this and that, we destroy the superorganism, the coming together of everything within a moment as it merges into something bigger than the mere sum of its parts. This emergent property is called life. To live, we must let the Self go. There is no One living; there is only living. One moment experienced this way is worth more than a thousand years lived otherwise.

Epilogue

Law is a big part of our life, but it is just that: one part. The skills we acquire as a lawyer should not become the tools that dismantle our house. Life cannot be controlled, analyzed, solved, or negotiated—life must be lived. For this, we must allow ourselves to become students of a world of wonder and interconnectedness.

As we sit here, we find solace in knowing that when we were born, we were endowed with the ability to see life for what it truly is—beautiful! We were blessed with the wisdom to cut through the noise and see into the heart of things. For this, we depend on no one and nothing. All we need to do is look straight at it.